TIBULLUS: *ELEGIES*

EDITED AND TRANSLATED BY GUY LEE

Published by Guy Lee, St John's College, Cambridge

Introduction, Translation and Notes © GUY LEE 1975

0 9504029 0 7

Designed and printed by Sebastian Carter at
The Rampant Lions Press, Cambridge

Printed and made in Great Britain

CONTENTS

ACKNOWLEDGEMENTS

My thanks are due to Dr A. Paredi of the Biblioteca Ambrosiana for kind permission to base my text on the Ambrosian MS, and to Mr W. A. Camps for generously allowing me to make use of his unpublished commentary on Tibullus.

I also wish to thank the following, who have helped me in various ways: Mr J. A. Crook, Miss J. M. Gilmartin, Dr N. F. M. Henry, Miss P. D. Huskinson, Sir Joseph Hutchinson, Prof. H. H. Huxley, Prof. G. Luck, Mr R. E. Thoday, Prof. K. D. White, and above all Helen Lee.

St John's College, Cambridge

INTRODUCTION

The reader who comes to Tibullus from the love poetry of Ovid will be surprised to discover in parts of his work a distinctly Ovidian tone. The *Consultation with Priapus* (1.4) in which the grotesque fertility god treats the poet to a brief lecture on the art of pederasty in elegantly balanced couplets is evidently intended to shock and to amuse and its unexpected conclusion to raise a laugh or at any rate a smile. On the formal side also the fact that no fewer than forty of the poem's forty-two pentameters end in a word of two syllables, a proportion un-paralleled in the first book of Propertius, the immediate predecessor of Tibullus's first collection – this fact only serves to strengthen the Ovidian impression made by the tone of the poem as a whole. Further, of the two exceptions to the disyllabic majority both in their different ways are justified by point. What is more, one of the two couplets concerned displays a feature without parallel in the whole of the output of Propertius, anticipating a device which is particularly associated with Ovid:

> Pieridas, pueri, doctos et amate poetas,
> aurea nec superent munera Pieridas.

> Love the Muses, O ye striplings, & the scholar poets,
> nor value gifts of gold above the Muses.

The structure of this couplet, with the Greek name of the Muses beginning the hexameter and ending the pentameter like an echo, is clearly meant to exemplify the poetic *doctrina* which the couplet itself explicitly recommends. Ovid in the *Amores* pushes this Tibullan idea a stage further when he mints the analogous couplet

> Militat omnis amans et habet sua castra Cupido:
> Attice, crede mihi, militat omnis amans.

> Lovers are soldiers all – in Cupid's private army.
> Atticus, take it from me – lovers are soldiers all.

But when Tibullus published his first collection in 27 or 26 BC, Ovid was a youth of sixteen, still attending the lectures of Porcius Latro and Arellius Fuscus in the school of rhetoric. It follows therefore that what we have called the Ovidian tone originates in Latin poetry with Tibullus. The wit, the grace, the easy and natural flow, the subdivision of the elegiac couplet into smaller self-contained units, sometimes as many as four, the predominance of the disyllabic ending to the pentameter, the relatively frequent enjambment or running on of the hexameter into the first or second foot of the pentameter – all these Ovidian features are already present in the elegiacs of Tibullus, who should accordingly be regarded as an important metrical innovator. Ovid was aware of his debt and repaid it at the age of twenty-four by writing a fine funeral elegy on the death of his master.

But the Ovidian tone, in the sense of light wit and elegance of manner, is only a part of what this nowadays much underrated poet has to offer. Though always 'polished and discriminating', *tersus atque elegans* (the words of Quintilian, who regards him as the best of the Latin elegists), Tibullus is more often serious than the Ovid of the amatory poems. He expresses, I believe, a wider range of feeling: humour and high spirits on occasion, as we have seen, but nostalgia too and melancholy, tenderness (his favourite adjective is *tener*) and compassion, fear, hatred, admiration, reverence – the list is incomplete; enough to say that if Propertius is the poet of passion and Ovid of wit, Tibullus is the poet of feeling. Granted that such labels are over-simplifications likely to mislead, that it is impossible to pin down any poet with a single blunt word, still they may serve perhaps as provisional pointers, aids to the sorting out of inarticulate impressions.

Three examples may help to make clearer something of the quality I am trying to express. First, Tibullan melancholy:

> Ibitis Aegaeas sine me, Messalla, per undas,
>   o utinam memores ipse cohorsque mei!
> me tenet ignotis aegrum Phaeacia terris,
>   abstineas auidas Mors modo nigra manus.

> Alas, Messalla, you will sail Aegean seas without me,
>   you & the company, but not, please God, forgetting
> the sick man, captive in Phaeacia, land of the unknown –
>   if only the Black Goddess withholds her grasping hand.

The poet appeals directly for our sympathy. His situation in real life, ill in bed somewhere in Corfu (for which the accepted name was then Corcyra), is transposed into the world of mythology, for Phaeacia was the mysterious island where the shipwrecked Odysseus swam ashore on the last stage of his long journey home to Ithaca. The Alexandrian poet Callimachus had identified it with Corcyra, but this identification was not accepted by the geographers and the island's real position (if it ever had one) unknown: hence one of the shades of meaning in *ignotis* here, a touch of subdued wit which helps to avoid self-pity. In each couplet grave slower-moving statement is followed by emotive dactylic exclamation; there is also contrast between *me tenet* and *ibitis, terris* and *undas*, compound *abstineas* and simple *tenet*. The lines are noticeably musical, have an almost hypnotic quality, largely owing perhaps to the diphthong *æ* and the long vowels *a* and *i*, which combined together in this context are suggestive of sorrow. I do not think these two couplets could be mistaken for the work of the younger Ovid or Propertius, though they anticipate the tone of Ovid's *Tristia*.

Secondly, a fine expression of that feeling of elation and invulnerability experienced at times by the young lover when Nature has played her age-old trick upon him and he 'walks on air', convinced that he bears a charmed life and that all is for the best in the best of all possible worlds:

> quisquis amore tenetur eat tutusque sacerque
> > qualibet; insidias non timuisse decet.
> non mihi pigra nocent hibernae frigora noctis,
> > non mihi cum multa decidit imber aqua.
> non labor hic laedit, reseret modo Delia postes
> > et uocet ad digiti me taciturna sonum.

> The love-possessed are sacred, safe to wander where they will;
> > to fear no ambush is their privilege.
> In the freezing winter night no frost can bite me;
> > no rain can damp me though it falls in floods.
> No harm in present hardship if my Delia turns the lock
> > & calls me silently – with one click of her finger.

The Latin lines have a lift about them that is partly the result of the predominantly dactylic movement, a sense of special individual magic that is partly due to the repetition, or anaphora (to use the technical term), of *non mihi . . . non mihi . . . non . . .*, and at the same time a gaiety that betrays itself in the word-play of *nocent . . . noctis* and the paradox of *uocet . . . taciturna*. Though the passage is closer to Ovid than to Propertius, it is still, I believe, unmistakably Tibullan.

The third example brings alive for the reader the feeling of tension followed by relief at two characteristic moments in the course of a clandestine affair:

> haec mihi te adducit tenebris multoque timore
> > coniungit nostras clam taciturna manus.
> haec foribusque manet noctu me affixa, proculque
> > cognoscit strepitus me ueniente pedum.

> In the dark she leads you to me & though terrified
>   stealthily with no word spoken joins our hands.
> Pressed to the door at night, she listens, waiting for me,
>   can recognise, far off, approaching steps as mine.

The first couplet conveys excitement, a sense of difficulty perhaps in the doubled consonants of *adducit tenebris* and of groping danger in the separation of *nostras* from *manus* by the monosyllabic adverb and the longer adjective. In the second hexameter the feeling of expectation is heightened by the pause after *affixa*, a word which pictures her as not only glued to the door but also intent on listening. The listening is further emphasised by the slight pause after *proculque*; then she recognises one sound in particular: he's coming – that's his footstep.

As regards the structure of a Tibullan poem, here again feeling is the deciding factor. Ovid, as is well known, constructs his elegies in a linear fashion, giving them an argumentative or narrative thread on which he keeps a pretty firm grip throughout. For example, the poem which starts with the echo couplet quoted above goes on to develop a point by point comparison of the lover and the soldier designed to prove that love is quite as strenuous and demanding as war; next proceeds to show that love has the highest military authority, for the greatest heroes of the *Iliad* and even the War-god himself were lovers; then maintains that love has toughened the poet, raised his morale and kept him busy; and finally advises all who want an active life to take up love. Tibullus on the other hand is more devious. The very transpositions that scholars from the time of Scaliger until late in the nineteenth century introduced into his text are themselves evidence that poetic structure with him is not a logical thing, not perhaps even a rational thing (though there is always good reason behind it), but rather an intentional avoidance of the obvious and the straightforward in favour of something more subtle and supple. His poems tend to grow rather than move forward – to grow by a proliferation of short sections expressing various related and contrasted moods. These sections quite often take the form of wishes or prayers, and the connexions between them, though discoverable on reflexion, are not always explicit. The whole poem is often held together by the repetition of certain key words and phrases that embody the main ideas with which the poem is concerned. To make this last point clear I must ask the reader to turn to the tenth poem of the first book and examine the following repetitions there: 2 *ferreus* and 59 *ferrum*; 4 *dirae Mortis* and 33 *atram . . . Mortem*; 7 *bella*, 33 *bellis* and 53 *Veneris bella*; 11–2 *tristia . . . arma* and 49–50 *tristia . . . arma*; 15 *aluistis*, 47 *aluit* and 67 *alma*; 22 *spicea* and 67 *spicam*; 45 *Pax candida* and 67–8 *Pax . . . candidus*. These seven seem to me the most important repetitions, but there are at least a dozen more that any interested reader can discover for himself, not counting such related words as 7 *faginus* and 20 *ligneus*, which also play their part in building up the Tibullan unity. Here too, in structure, as also in metre, we find that Tibullus shows marked originality.

If however the individual poem seems to grow to its completion, the relative placing of the ten poems that make up Book One is clearly the result of careful calculation. The first and the tenth go together as giving the poet's philosophy of life, if that is not too grand a phrase to use of such an unsystematic thinker as Tibullus. In between these two, which serve as introduction and conclusion to the collection, are placed three pairs of poems, each pair separated from the next by a single contrasting poem on a different theme. Thus, the second and third poems, about Delia, are separated from the fifth and sixth on the same subject, by the consultation with Priapus on homosexual love, a poem contrasting in treatment, tone and theme with the heterosexual pair on either side of it. Similarly the fifth and sixth, about Delia, are separated from the eighth and ninth, about Marathus, by the birthday poem for Messalla, which in its turn makes a complete contrast in tone and theme with its surroundings. Again, the two members of each of the three pairs, though all alike in being about love unfulfilled, nevertheless contrast with one another: for example, in the second poem the lovers are separated by the guard set on Delia by her absent husband; in the third they are separated by war, the poet being on his way to the Near East on the staff of Messalla and taken ill, as we have seen above.

The second book is roughly half the length of the first and consists of only six poems. These, though contrasted with one another in a similar way, taken together leave an impression of incompletion. This book lacks the evident unity of the first; it has not been fully achieved and at the same time is unusually short for a collection of elegies. We are therefore probably right to infer that it was unfinished when Tibullus died and published posthumously by his executor. He died young in 19 or 18 BC, shortly after Virgil, as we gather from a contemporary epigram by the poet Domitius Marsus, which will be found on p. 96. Precisely how young we can only guess, but according to Varro a man could be called *iuuenis* from the age of thirty to the age of forty-five.

Of his life we know little more than can be gleaned from these two books of elegies. Admittedly there is a *Vita* or brief biography (printed on p. 96) which appears in some of his manuscripts and which on linguistic evidence can be said to derive from the work of Suetonius, *De Poetis*, written considerably more than a century after the poet's death. But this as it stands contains nothing that could not have been gathered by inference from the elegies themselves, from the epigram of Domitius Marsus, which it quotes, and, finally, from the verse epistle of Horace (*Epist.* 1.4) to the elegiac poet Albius, who in antiquity, as today, was taken to be one and the same as Albius Tibullus. His *praenomen* or first name is not recorded.

He was a Roman knight and owned a small estate in Latium, on which he was born – a fact which makes him one of the very few truly Latin poets, as opposed to Italians like Horace and Ovid, or provincials like Catullus and Virgil. His patron was the soldier, statesman and orator Marcus Valerius Messalla Corvinus (64 BC to AD 8), distinguished member of an ancient patrician family, famous too as a literary purist. In the troubled times of the Civil Wars Messalla steered a prudential course, first supporting Brutus and Cassius, then after their defeat at Philippi (where he commanded the victorious right wing of their army) transferring his support to Antony, later still attaching himself to Octavian, with whom he was Consul in 31 BC and took part in the battle of Actium. It is remarkable, by the way, that Tibullus, Messalla's protégé, unlike the other Augustan poets nowhere in his elegies refers to the Caesar. The omission must be intentional; whether it implies a slight is open to argument, but certainly it indicates a conservative loyalty, in the tradition of the old Republic, to his own aristocratic patron.

He fought under Messalla's command as a military tribune in Gaul and was awarded, so the *Vita* informs us, military decorations, *militaria dona* (but this *may* be an inference extorted from 1.7.9 *non sine me tibi partus honos* 'not without me was your glory gained'). He accompanied Messalla on his expedition to the Levant, but fell ill on the way; whether he rejoined the expeditionary force on his recovery is uncertain, though he writes in 1.7 with some knowledge of Cilicia, Syro-Palestine and Egypt.

The Delia celebrated in his first collection, blonde and blue-eyed, as we gather from 1.5.43–6, is said by Apuleius, almost two centuries later, to have been in real life named Plania. If this is true two consequences follow: her Greek pseudonym is a translation of her Latin gentile name, for the Latin adjective *planus* is equivalent to the Greek *delos*; and secondly, she was a *ciuis Romana*, for only Roman citizens bore gentile names. In 1.6 she has a 'husband' (*coniunx*), to whom she is not in the full Roman sense married, because she does not wear the traditional dress of a Roman *matrona*; therefore she is the man's concubine and probably also a freedwoman, or *libertina*, manumitted by (and perhaps the concubine of) her former master, for it is rather improbable that a free-born *ciuis Romana* in Equestrian Society would consent to concubinage.

The poet's liaison with Delia ended at some date after the publication of Book One. In Book Two he is in love with a woman he calls Nemesis, but as we have no word about her from Apuleius or any other source we are left to speculate on his reason for choosing this ill-omened name for Delia's successor. Nemesis is the Greek goddess of Retribution; Catullus calls her *uemens dea* 'a passionate goddess' and perhaps Tibullus has this description in mind. She is thought of as ready to pounce on anyone who 'talks big' and in particular as the avenger of slighted lovers. In the Greek Anthology there is an epigram (12.140) describing how Nemesis punished the anonymous author for decrying the good looks of a certain boy by making him fall madly in love with the boy; this epigram is imitated by Meleager (12.141), the anthologist of the famous *Garland*, which was available in Italy early in the first century BC. It is an epigram that may well have been known to Tibullus, who elsewhere shows a good knowledge of Greek poetry and very likely of the *Garland* itself (see note on 1.2.29–30). So we may perhaps guess that he had at one time thought poorly of the girl he calls Nemesis and later found himself infatuated by her. Some scholars, it is true, have regarded her as a literary figure merely, with no real existence; but this means that we must also regard as pure fiction the extraordinary passage in 2.6 about her little sister, who fell to her death from an upper window. The incredulity of some modern literati is itself a phenomenon beyond belief.

And belief is Tibullus's most endearing characteristic. He believes in the gods; he half believes in magic; he believes in an idealized past and a happy future; he believes in Delia, Marathus, Nemesis; but above all he believes in the traditional religious rituals:

> Nam ueneror seu stipes habet desertus in agris
>   seu uetus in triuio florida serta lapis.

> For I pray at every solitary tree-stump in the fields
>   or old stone at the crossways that is garlanded with flowers.

One is surprised to meet this couplet at the start of a collection of love elegies. It reminds one of Virgil's admonition at *Georgics* 1.338 *in primis uenerare deos* 'first and foremost worship the Gods' and can at the same time be regarded as a deliberate contradiction of Lucretius 5.1198–9

15   *Introduction*

> Nec pietas ullast uelatum saepe uideri
> uertier ad lapidem

> And there is no piety in being often seen
> with head covered turning towards a stone.

Again, a little later in the same elegy one meets the following couplet:

> Adsitis, diui, neu uos e paupere mensa
> dona nec e puris spernite fictilibus.

> O Gods, vouchsafe your presence & do not scorn the gifts
> from a poor man's table & spotless earthenware.

The reader of Propertius and Ovid is unprepared for this simple and direct expression of religious feeling. Critics can talk of literary *topoi*, the poet's *persona*, the intentional or the documentary fallacy, but all the same the common reader senses at these points, as he senses when reading Wordsworth, that the poet is telling the truth about himself, that his feeling for religion is genuine and indeed basic to his character.

At the centre of this religion stand the homely Lares, guardian spirits of hearth and farm, depicted in art as young men dressed in short tunics, holding above their heads a wine-bowl or a drinking-horn, and very often dancing. Their images were placed beside the hearth and worshipped with offerings of food and wine, incense and flowers. These are the gods addressed in the quotation above and requested not to despise the gifts from the poet's simple table. They are never mentioned in the first book of Propertius, never mentioned in the three books of Ovid's *Amores*, but their name occurs five times in Book One and four times in Book Two of Tibullus. Altogether he devotes some thirty lines to them, promising them sacrifices and offerings of incense, undertaking to wear the myrtle in their honour, mentioning their ancient images of wood inherited from his ancestors, and praying for their protection on the field of battle:

> Sed patrii seruate Lares: aluistis et idem
> cursarem uestros cum tener ante pedes.

> Save me, Lares of my fathers, as you nurtured me
> when I ran around in childhood at your feet.

This simple but vivid reminiscence of his childhood, employing incidentally a verb (*cursare*) which occurs nowhere else in the whole of Latin elegy, is typical of his backward-looking cast of mind and very appealing. We suspect that there is a similar autobiographical touch in his finest poem of all, the first of the second book, when he tells us that

it was a country child who first made a garland of spring flowers as a
chaplet for the Lares; he himself in childhood had probably done the
same. Certainly from his earliest years he will have witnessed or taken
part in the ancient annual ceremony with which that poem opens –
the ceremony of the purification of the fields and crops by 'going about'
them in solemn white-robed procession, and he will have heard his
father speaking the traditional form of prayer whose distant echo still
lingers in the couplet

> Di patrii, purgamus agros, purgamus agrestes:
>   uos mala de nostris pellite limitibus.

> Gods of our fathers, we purge the fields & the field-workers:
>   drive away all evil from our boundaries.

And, as the commentators tell us, among the *di patrii* the Lares would
hold an important place as guardians of the family estate and its
bounds.

Tibullus's evident respect for the ancestors, his nostalgia for an
idealized past when life was simple, gods wooden and men honest, his
love of the country and its seasonal ritual round of labour and religious
observance, these habitual attitudes owe at least as much to the Lares
as they do to his military experience under Messalla in the civil war or
to the worst excesses of the economic boom that began with the return
of peace to the Roman world. Even Catullus, the 'urbane' provincial
for whom urban Rome had been home and life, who regarded the
country as crude and witless (*rus inficetum*), fit stamping-ground for
goat-milkers and clodhoppers – even Catullus could appreciate the
beauty of his estate at Sirmione when he returned to his *Lar Familiaris*
from foreign service in Bithynia. But Tibullus was no provincial. Born
in Latium, near enough to Rome not to want to live there, with no
desire to shine in the smart set of the capital, he had served in Gaul
and perhaps in the Near East: to such a man his family home in the
country, seen in imagination from a legionary tent among the Aquitani
or from distant and mountainous Cilicia, must have appeared a small
earthly paradise, under the protection of the familiar Lares.

Propertius in a mood of lovelorn gloom retires to a lonely grove, the
property of Zephyrus, to carve the name of Cynthia on the bark of
beeches, and of pines too (perhaps a more difficult operation this), to
pour out his complaint to the woods and rocks and hear them echo her
name as Virgil's bucolic woods had echoed the name of Amaryllis.
But the country celebrated by Tibullus in a number of his poems is no
Arcadian landscape. It is the countryside of Latium, of the *regio*

Pedana, a few miles east of Rome, where cereals and wine are the chief crops, pigs and sheep the chief livestock, where at vintage-time the grapes are trodden in portable boat-shaped vats (*lintres*), where the daily work is hard and where festivals are looked forward to as days of well-earned rest from labour. Of course the picture is somewhat idealized, as it also is in the *Georgics* of Virgil, but it is firmly based on the realities of the way of life into which he was born and for which he retained a lifelong affection, nourished by that deeper affection for the gods who presided over it.

To these gods he attributes the origin of civilisation and the arts. House-building, the domestication of animals, the invention of the wheel, agriculture, spinning and weaving were their gifts to man; the arts of music, song, dance and poetry originated in their worship, invented by country people as expressions of individual and communal supplication and thanksgiving. He is pleased to call himself *rusticus*, giving the word (which carries strong overtones of boorishness) a positive value lacking in its use by Ovid and Propertius. He regards the small sheepfarmer as a greater hero than the valiant soldier: the sheepfarmer too fights for a living, but constructively; he represents stability, continuity, the simple, useful life. Peace is the natural human condition. Peace, one might say, is the greatest of the country gods, for the civilisation that they gave the human race depends on her.

But in 2.1 the list of country gods and origins ends with Cupid:

> Ipse quoque inter agros interque armenta Cupido
>   natus et indomitas dicitur inter equas . . .
> a miseri quos hic grauiter deus urget; at ille
>   felix cui placidus leniter afflat Amor.
> sancte, ueni dapibus festis, sed pone sagittas
>
>   et procul ardentes hinc, precor, abde faces.
> Cupid himself, in fable, was born among the fields,
>   among the cattle & the wild mares . . .
> Wretched are they, alas, on whom this god bears hard,
>   but happy he who feels Love's breath serene.
> Come, Holy One, attend our feast, but lay aside your arrows
>   & far away, I pray you, hide your blazing torch.

Again the religious tone is very marked. True, Catullus had called Cupid *sancte puer*, but the emphasis on the god's boyhood detracts a little, perhaps, from the force of the adjective and conjures up a mental picture of the putti of the Pompeian frescoes. In the Tibullan context, however, despite the conventional arrows and torches, the impression made is that of a more powerful and elemental figure than the Alexandrian boy-god, a force ambivalent and irresistible, ruling the world of beasts and men. Only once does Tibullus directly call Cupid *puer* – in the last poem of Book Two. In fact it is not until Book Two that he uses the name Cupid at all – and then only three times; in Book One, and elsewhere in Book Two, he refers to the god as Amor.

Book One indeed is remarkable for the general picture it presents of love as a positive moral force, a force contrasting strongly with the destructive passion attacked in the fourth book of Lucretius and of Cicero's *Tusculans* and realised so vividly in the first elegy of Propertius. The majestic figure of Venus predominates. She rules from high Olympus. Though merciful to her servants yet as the daughter of blood and raging sea she takes vengeance on those who sin against her in word or deed. She teaches her worshippers through suffering and rewards them with an after-life in Elysium. She helps the brave but demands of them reverence, secrecy and kindness. She punishes the mockers, the tale-bearers, the hard-hearted, above all those who break faith for mercenary reasons:

> Si quis diuitiis captus uiolauit amorem,
>   asperaque est illi difficilisque Venus.

> If anyone for money does violence to love,
>   Venus is hard on him and difficult.

Clearly the pentameter has a double meaning: Venus is at the same time the goddess of love and the sex-life over which she rules; the Latin *asperaque est illi* means 'rough *for* him' as well as 'rough *on* him'. But more interesting here is the concept of the violation of love. *Violare* is a strong word with implications not only of physical violence but of religious desecration and spiritual defilement. Tibullus is unique in his application of this word to love; he uses it five times in Book One, always in an erotic context – clear evidence of his religious attitude towards love at this stage in his poetic career. This attitude is very different from the down-to-earth view of love presented by Ovid in his celebration of *Love's Triumph* (*Amores* 1.2):

> Mens Bona ducetur manibus post terga retortis
>   et Pudor et castris quidquid Amoris obest . . .
> Blanditiae comites tibi erunt Errorque Furorque,
>   adsidue partes turba secuta tuas.

his tu militibus superas hominesque deosque;
    haec tibi si demas commoda, nudus eris.
laeta triumphanti de summo mater Olympo
    plaudet et adpositas sparget in ora rosas.

Conscience & Common Sense & all Love's enemies
    will be dragged along with hands tied behind their backs . . .
Your loyal irregulars Flattery Passion & Illusion
    will act as bodyguard,
the forces that bring you victory over gods & men,
    providing cover for your nakedness.
Your laughing mother will watch the Triumph from Olympus
    and clap her hands and shower you with roses.

Ovid the reductionist here strips off love's mystery, leaving the god denuded and open to epicurean management by the clear-sighted reason. His more maternal and decorative Venus, though she too watches the scene from the summit of Olympus, is content to scatter roses and forget about revenge.

In the first two poems of Book Two love still retains a religious aura, but thereafter the point of view changes completely. Like Catullus in the final stage of his affair with Lesbia, Tibullus now looks on love as a disease, but (here, though, unlike Catullus) a disease whose pain can actually be enjoyable:

Et faueo morbo – quin iuuat ipse dolor.

Clinging to my sickness, finding pleasure in the pain.

Alternatively he describes love as a form of slavery, using for once a long mythological example to illustrate the point, the story of how Apollo, god of poetry, prophecy and medicine, fell in love with the young Admetus and served as herdsman on his farm, living in a shack, his passion unrequited. But just as Tibullus accepts the disease, so he accepts love's slavery, though not of course without complaint. He is prepared to put up with the avarice of Nemesis as a fact inevitable in an avaricious society. He is even prepared to turn the tables on Venus herself, by robbing her temples to get the means to buy gifts for his mistress:

Aut rapiam suspensa sacris insignia fanis:
    sed Venus ante alios est uiolanda mihi.
illa malum facinus suadet dominamque rapacem
    dat mihi: sacrilegas sentiat illa manus.

> Or I'll steal the sacred offerings hung up on temple walls:
>   and Venus shall be first to be profaned.
> She tempts me to do evil & devotes me to a grasping
>   mistress: she deserves to suffer sacrilege.

The situation is paradoxical: he himself is now willing to desecrate true love (the very thing he maintained in Book One that Venus would inevitably punish) by buying Nemesis' affection. Venus has been demythologised and the sinister figure of Nemesis deified in her place; the worship of Amor is now subjected to her conditions. Yes, for her the poet would even sell his estate and part with the ancestral Lares (another complete reversal of his attitude in Book One):

> illius est nobis lege colendus Amor.
> quin etiam sedes iubeat si uendere auitas,
>   ite sub imperium sub titulumque, Lares.

> Love's worship means obedience to her laws.
> Why, even if she bade me sell my ancestral home,
>   I'd pack the Lares off under a bill of sale.

But nevertheless in this cycle of poems to Nemesis the attitude to love is still positive; the suffering is still worthwhile. What makes it worthwhile is Hope. The poet signs off suddenly, leaving the reader with Love (unfulfilled) and Hope, and with the strong impression that in the long run Hope is the higher value.*

* I acknowledge a debt to W. Heilmann's unpublished dissertation *Die Bedeutung der Venus bei Tibull*, Frankfurt am Main, 1959.

ALBI TIBVLLI ELEGIARVM
LIBER PRIMVS

ALBIUS TIBULLUS: *ELEGIES*
BOOK ONE

I

DIVITIAS alius fuluo sibi congerat auro
     et teneat culti iugera magna soli,
quem labor assiduus uicino terreat hoste,
     Martia cui somnos classica pulsa fugent:
me mea paupertas uitae traducat inerti,
     dum meus assiduo luceat igne focus.

Ipse seram teneras maturo tempore uites
     rusticus et facili grandia poma manu,
nec Spes destituat, sed frugum semper aceruos
     praebeat et pleno pinguia musta lacu: 10
nam ueneror seu stipes habet desertus in agris
     seu uetus in triuio florida serta lapis,
et quodcumque mihi pomum nouus educat annus
     libatum agricolam ponitur ante deum.

Flaua Ceres, tibi sit nostro de rure corona
     spicea quae templi pendeat ante fores,
pomosisque ruber custos ponatur in hortis
     terreat ut saeua falce Priapus aues.
uos quoque, felicis quondam, nunc pauperis agri
     custodes, fertis munera uestra, Lares;   20
tunc uitula innumeros lustrabat caesa iuuencos,
     nunc agna exigui est hostia parua soli:
agna cadet uobis, quam circum rustica pubes
     clamet 'io, messes et bona uina date'.

Iam modo, iam possim contentus uiuere paruo
     nec semper longae deditus esse uiae,
sed Canis aestiuos ortus uitare sub umbra
     arboris ad riuos praetereuntis aquae.
nec tamen interdum pudeat tenuisse bidentem
     aut stimulo tardos increpuisse boues;   30
non agnamue sinu pigeat fetumue capellae
     desertum oblita matre referre domum.

At uos exiguo pecori, furesque lupique,
     parcite: de magno est praeda petenda grege.
hic ego pastoremque meum lustrare quotannis
     et placidam soleo spargere lacte Palem.

Wealth let others gather for themselves in yellow gold
and acquire great acres of cultivated land –
scared on active service, in contact with the enemy,
their sleep put to flight by the blare of trumpet-calls.
But let my general poverty transfer *me* to inaction,
so long as fire glows always in my hearth.

Early in the season I should set the tender vines
and the tall maidens with a peasant's practised hand.
Hope would never fail me, but deliver an abundance
of produce, brimming over the vat at vintage time.
For I pray at every solitary tree-stump in the fields
or old stone at the cross-roads that is garlanded with flowers;
and the first of every fruit the new season raises for me
is offered at the feet of the farmer God.

For you, O golden Ceres, my land would bear a crown
of wheaten spikes to hang on your temple door.
I'd place a red Priapus to stand sentry in the orchard
and scare away the birds with his reaping-hook.
You, O Lares, also receive your gifts as guardians
of a property once prosperous, now poor:
once a slaughtered heifer purified uncounted steers;
now my little acres offer a ewe-lamb.
The ewe-lamb shall be yours and at her sacrifice the peasants
can shout 'O Lares, grant us good harvest and good wine'.

If only, now at last, I can live content with little
and not be handed over to the never-ending road,
but avoid the summer rising of the Dog-star, in the shadow
of a tree, beside the waters of a running stream!
Not that I would be ashamed to wield a mattock sometimes
or reprimand the slow oxen with a goad,
nor would I be too civilised to bring home in my arms
a lamb or kid abandoned by a careless mother.

But let the robber and the wolf spare my little flock
and plunder the big folds,
for here I never fail to purify my shepherd
and sprinkle kindly Pales every year with milk.

adsitis, diui, neu uos e paupere mensa
    dona nec e puris spernite fictilibus:
fictilia antiquus primum sibi fecit agrestis,
    pocula de facili composuitque luto.   40

Non ego diuitias patrum fructusque requiro
    quos tulit antiquo condita messis auo:
parua seges satis est, satis est requiescere lecto
    si licet et solito membra leuare toro.
quam iuuat immites uentos audire cubantem
    et dominam tenero continuisse sinu!
aut gelidas hibernus aquas cum fuderit Auster,
    securum somnos igne iuuante sequi!
hoc mihi contingat: sit diues iure furorem
    qui maris et tristes ferre potest pluuias.   50

O quantum est auri pereat potiusque smaragdi
    quam fleat ob nostras ulla puella uias!
te bellare decet terra, Messalla, marique
    ut domus hostiles praeferat exuuias:
me retinent uinctum formosae uincla puellae,
    et sedeo duras ianitor ante fores.

Non ego laudari curo, mea Delia; tecum
    dum modo sim, quaeso segnis inersque uocer.
te spectem suprema mihi cum uenerit hora;
    te teneam moriens deficiente manu.   60
flebis et arsuro positum me, Delia, lecto,
    tristibus et lacrimis oscula mixta dabis.
flebis: non tua sunt duro praecordia ferro
    uincta, nec in tenero stat tibi corde silex.
illo non iuuenis poterit de funere quisquam,
    lumina non uirgo sicca referre domum.
tu manes ne laede meos, sed parce solutis
    crinibus et teneris, Delia, parce genis.

Interea, dum Fata sinunt, iungamus amores:
    iam ueniet tenebris Mors adoperta caput;   70
iam subrepet iners aetas, neque amare decebit,
    dicere nec cano blanditias capite.
nunc leuis est tractanda Venus, dum frangere postes
    non pudet et rixas inseruisse iuuat.

O Gods, vouchsafe your presence, and do not scorn the gifts
from a poor man's table and spotless earthenware:
earthenware was the invention of a countryman
long ago, who shaped cups from pliant clay.

I do not miss the fortune of my father or the profit
that garnered harvest brought my grandfather of old.
Enough is a small crop, enough is sleeping in a bed
and lightening the limbs on the familiar couch.
How pleasant lying there at night to listen to wild winds
and contain a mistress in tender embrace!
Or when the wintry southern gale slings down the freezing sleet,
to pursue sleep in safety, aided by a fire:
Let this be my good fortune: I resign the right to wealth
to those who can endure sad rain and raging sea.

O perish all the gold and every emerald in the world
sooner than any girl weep as we march away!
It is right that you, Messalla, campaign by land and sea
to adorn your town-house with the spoils of war.
But I am held a pris'ner, fettered by a lovely girl,
and take my post as keeper at her cruel door.

Glory has no charms for me, my Delia. They can call me
slack and ineffective, if only I'm with you.
O let me gaze at you, when my last hour comes –
hold you, as I die, in my failing grasp!
Delia, you will weep for me laid on the bed of burning
and you will give me kisses mixed with bitter tears.
Yes, you will weep: your heart is not encased in iron
nor is there flint in your tender breast.
There will be no young man and no unmarried girl
going home dry-eyed from my funeral.
But do no violence, Delia, to my departed spirit:
spare your flowing tresses and spare your tender cheeks.

Meanwhile, with Fate's permission, let us unite and love.
Tomorrow Death will come, head hooded – in the dark,
or useless Age creep up, and it will not be seemly
to make white-headed love or pretty speeches.
Light Venus is our duty now, while there is no disgrace
in breaking down a door, while brawling brings delight.

hic ego dux milesque bonus. uos, signa tubaeque,
    ite procul; cupidis uulnera ferte uiris,
ferte et opes: ego composito securus aceruo
    dites despiciam despiciamque famem.

II

Adde merum uinoque nouos compesce dolores,
    occupet ut fessi lumina uicta sopor;
neu quisquam multo percussum tempora Baccho
    excitet, infelix dum requiescit amor:
nam posita est nostrae custodia saeua puellae,
    clauditur et dura ianua firma sera.

Ianua difficilis domini, te uerberet imber,
    te Iouis imperio fulmina missa petant.
ianua, iam pateas uni mihi, uicta querelis,
    neu furtim uerso cardine aperta sones;   10
et mala siqua tibi dixit dementia nostra,
    ignoscas: capiti sint precor illa meo.
te meminisse decet quae plurima uoce peregi
    supplice, cum posti florida serta darem.

Tu quoque, ne timide custodes, Delia, falle;
    audendum est: fortes adiuuat ipsa Venus.
illa fauet seu quis iuuenis noua limina temptat
    seu reserat fixo dente puella fores.
illa docet furtim molli decedere lecto,
    illa pedem nullo ponere posse sono,   20
illa uiro coram nutus conferre loquaces
    blandaque compositis abdere uerba notis;
nec docet hoc omnes sed quos nec inertia tardat
    nec uetat obscura surgere nocte timor.

En ego cum tenebris tota uagor anxius urbe
    ·   ·   ·   ·   ·   ·   ·   ·   ·
nec sinit occurrat quisquam qui corpora ferro
    uulneret aut rapta praemia ueste petat.
quisquis amore tenetur eat tutusque sacerque
    qualibet; insidias non timuisse decet.   30
non mihi pigra nocent hibernae frigora noctis,
    non mihi cum multa decidit imber aqua;

Here I can lead & soldier well. Eagles & trumpets, dismiss!
Bring wounds to greedy husbands, and bring them money too.
But let me live at peace myself, with produce heaped in store,
looking down on hunger as I look down on the rich.

2

Pour it neat, boy. Discipline fresh misery with drink,
letting sleep invade these tired defeated eyes,
and when the Wine-God in his strength has hit me on the temples
see that no one wakes me while unhappy love's at rest.
For now a cruel sentinel stands watch upon my girl
and her heavy door is shut and firmly barred.

O door, stubborn as your master, may the rainstorm lash you
and launched at Jove's command may flash of lightning blast you!
Please, door – open just for me, moved by my complaining.
But silence, as you swing on slowly turning hinge!
Forgive me if I cursed you in my infatuation.
Let the curses light on my own head.
It's right you should remember all my prayers and promises
when I hung those garlands of flowers on your post.

You too, Delia: be bold and trick the guard.
You must do and dare, for Venus helps the brave.
She favours the young man who reconnoitres a new threshold,
and the girl who opens a door with home-made key.
She teaches the withdrawal by stealth from the soft bed,
the inaudible positioning of feet,
the conference by nod in the presence of a husband,
concealment of sweet words in signals pre-arranged.
Her teaching's not for everyone but only those with courage
and capacity to rise in the shadow of the night.

Look, when in the dark I wander through the city streets distraught
·   ·   ·   ·   ·   ·   ·   ·   ·

and stops me meeting anyone who stabs you in the back
or steals clothes for a living.
The love-possessed are sacred, safe to wander where they will;
to fear no ambush is their privilege.
In the freezing winter's night no frost can bite me;
no rain can damp me though it falls in floods.

non labor hic laedit, reseret modo Delia postes
    et uocet ad digiti me taciturna sonum.

Parcite luminibus, seu uir seu femina fiat
    obuia; celari uult sua furta Venus.
ne strepitu terrete pedum neu quaerite nomen
    neu prope fulgenti lumina ferte face.
siquis et imprudens aspexerit, occulat ille
    perque deos omnes se meminisse neget;
nam fuerit quicumque loquax, is sanguine natam,
    is Venerem e rabido sentiet esse mari.

Nec tamen huic credet coniunx tuus, ut mihi uerax
    pollicita est magico saga ministerio.
hanc ego de caelo ducentem sidera uidi;
    fluminis haec rapidi carmine uertit iter;
haec cantu finditque solum manesque sepulcris
    elicit et tepido deuocat ossa rogo.
iam tenet infernas magico stridore cateruas;
    iam iubet aspersas lacte referre pedem.
cum libet, haec tristi depellit nubila caelo;
    cum libet, aestiuo conuocat orbe niues.
sola tenere malas Medeae dicitur herbas,
    sola feros Hecatae perdomuisse canes.

Haec mihi composuit cantus quis fallere posses;
    ter cane, ter dictis despue carminibus:
ille nihil poterit de nobis credere cuiquam,
    non sibi, si in molli uiderit ipse toro.
tu tamen abstineas aliis, nam cetera cernet
    omnia, de me uno sentiet ille nihil.
quid credam? nempe haec eadem se dixit amores
    cantibus aut herbis soluere posse meos,
et me lustrauit taedis, et nocte serena
    concidit ad magicos hostia pulla deos.
non ego totus abesset amor sed mutuus esset
    orabam, nec te posse carere uelim.

Ferreus ille fuit qui, te cum posset habere,
    maluerit praedas stultus et arma sequi.
ille licet Cilicum uictas agat ante cateruas,
    ponat et in capto Martia castra solo,

No harm in present hardship, if my Delia turns the lock
and calls me silently – with one click of her finger.

Male or female, should you meet me, look the other way:
the thefts of Love are secret – that is Venus' will.
Do not scare me with your footstep, do not ask my name
or shine your torches near me.
Any accidental witness is to hide the truth
and by all the gods deny his memory.
For every tell-tale shall be taught that Venus is the daughter
of blood and raging sea.

In any case your husband won't believe him, Delia;
for so an honest witch assured me by her magic.
I have seen her drawing down the stars from heaven.
Her chanting can reverse the river's flow.
Her spells can split the ground, lure ghosts from graves
and pluck the bones from smouldering pyres.
Now with magic wailing she holds the infernal troop;
now with sprinkled milk orders their return.
When she pleases she can drive the clouds from sullen skies;
when she pleases muster snow in summer's dome.
Only she, I'm told, knows all Medea's evil herbs;
only she can tame Hecate's fierce hounds.

She has written me a spell to enable you to trick him.
Speak it thrice and spit thrice when you have spoken.
He'll then believe no story anyone may tell of us –
not even his own eyes if he catches us in bed.
But keep away from other men. He'll see everything else.
I'm the only one he will never notice.
The same witch even promised, though it passes my belief,
by her spells or herbs to free me of my love.
She fumigated me with pitch-pine on a moonlit night
and slaughtered a black victim to the gods below.
I prayed that love be mutual, not absent altogether.
How could I ever wish to live without you?

Steel-hearted was the man who had you for the asking
but chose, the fool, to follow arms and plunder.
Let him drive Cilician prisoners in their crowds before him
and pitch his camp in captured territory

totus et argento contectus, totus et auro,
    insideat celeri conspiciendus equo:
ipse boues – mea si tecum modo Delia – possim
    iungere et in solito pascere monte pecus;
et te dum liceat teneris retinere lacertis,
    mollis et inculta sit mihi somnus humo.
quid Tyrio recubare toro sine amore secundo
    prodest, cum fletu nox uigilanda uenit?
nam neque tunc plumae nec stragula picta soporem
    nec sonitus placidae ducere possit aquae.   80

Num Veneris magnae uiolaui numina uerbo
    et mea nunc poenas impia lingua luit?
num feror incestus sedes adiisse deorum
    sertaque de sanctis deripuisse focis?
non ego, si merui, dubitem procumbere templis
    et dare sacratis oscula liminibus;
non ego tellurem genibus perrepere supplex
    et miserum sancto tundere poste caput.

At tu qui lentus rides mala nostra caueto.
    mox tibi, non uni saeuiet usque deus.   90
uidi ego qui iuuenum miseros lusisset amores
    post Veneris uinclis subdere colla senem,
et sibi blanditias tremula componere uoce,
    et manibus canas fingere uelle comas;
stare nec ante fores puduit caraeue puellae
    ancillam medio detinuisse foro.
hunc puer, hunc iuuenis turba circumterit arta,
    despuit in molles et sibi quisque sinus.

At mihi parce, Venus. semper tibi dedita seruit
    mens mea. quid messes uris acerba tuas?   100

III

Ibitis Aegaeas sine me, Messalla, per undas,
    o utinam memores, ipse cohorsque mei!
me tenet ignotis aegrum Phaeacia terris,
    abstineas auidas Mors modo nigra manus.
abstineas, Mors atra, precor: non hic mihi mater,
    quae legat in maestos ossa perusta sinus;

and cased from head to foot in gold and silver armour
parade before the public on his charger.
Myself, if I could only be with you, my Delia,
I'd yoke the oxen, feed the flock on the familiar hill.
So long as I could hold you prisoner in tender arms
my sleep would be soft on the natural ground.
What's the good of lying love-lorn on a purple couch
when night arrives with wakefulness and weeping?
For neither feathers then nor painted coverlets
nor sound of quiet water can bring sleep.

Has word of mine profaned the majesty of Venus
and is my tongue now paying the price of blasphemy?
Can I be accused of defiling the gods' temples
or of stealing garlands from their holy hearths?
If guilty I'd not hesitate to fall down on my face
in the porch and kiss the consecrated threshold,
to crawl in penance on my knees and beat my wretched head
against the holy door.

But let the man who heartlessly derides my woes beware.
His turn will come; the God won't punish me for ever.
I have seen the mocker of youth's unhappy love
as an old man yield his neck to Venus' chain,
practise pretty speeches in a quavering voice
and try with trembling hand to set his grizzled hair.
Nor was he ashamed to serenade his precious girl
and accost her maid in public in the Forum.
The young men and the children throng and thrust around him,
spitting in their tunics to avoid bad luck.

But, Venus, *my* devoted heart is ever at your service.
Have mercy. Why in rancour burn the harvest that is yours?

3

Alas, Messalla, you will sail Aegean seas without me –
you and the company – but not, please God, forgetting
the sick man, captive in Phaeacia, land of the unknown,
if only the Black Goddess withholds her grasping hand.
Dark Death, withhold, I pray you. I have no mother here
to gather up the calcined bones to her sad breast;

non soror, Assyrios cineri quae dedat odores
    et fleat effusis ante sepulcra comis;
Delia non usquam, quae me quam mitteret urbe
    dicitur ante omnes consuluisse deos.   10

Illa sacras pueri sortes ter sustulit: illi
    rettulit e trinis omina certa puer.
cuncta dabant reditus, tamen est deterrita nusquam
    quin fleret nostras respiceretque uias.
ipse ego, solator, cum iam mandata dedissem,
    quaerebam tardas anxius usque moras:
aut ego sum causatus aues aut omina dira
    Saturniue sacram me tenuisse diem.
o quotiens ingressus iter mihi tristia dixi
    offensum in porta signa dedisse pedem!   20
audeat inuito ne quis discedere amore
    aut sciet egressum se prohibente deo.

Quid tua nunc Isis mihi, Delia, quid mihi prosunt
    illa tua totiens aera repulsa manu,
quidue, pie dum sacra colis, pureque lauari
    te (memini) et puro secubuisse toro?
nunc, dea, nunc succurre mihi – nam posse mederi
    picta docet templis multa tabella tuis –
ut mea uotiuas persoluens Delia uoces
    ante sacras lino tecta fores sedeat   30
bisque die resoluta comas tibi dicere laudes
    insignis turba debeat in Pharia.
at mihi contingat patrios celebrare Penates
    reddereque antiquo menstrua tura Lari.

Quam bene Saturno uiuebant rege, priusquam
    tellus in longas est patefacta uias!
nondum caeruleas pinus contempserat undas,
    effusum uentis praebueratque sinum;
nec uagus ignotis repetens compendia terris
    presserat externa nauita merce ratem.   40
illo non ualidus subiit iuga tempore taurus,
    non domito frenos ore momordit equus;
non domus ulla fores habuit, non fixus in agris
    qui regeret certis finibus arua lapis;

no sister to bestow Assyrian perfumes on the ashes
and weep beside the grave with streaming hair;
no Delia – and yet, before she let me leave the city,
she sought at every temple counsel of the gods.

Thrice from the boy's urn she drew the sacred lots;
thrice out of three the boy saw favourable signs:
all promised safe return. But nothing could dissuade her
from weeping for regret of our long journey.
I too, her comforter, after the last farewell,
looked for postponement in despair
and made excuses, claiming that unlucky birds or omens
or Saturn's sacred day compelled my staying.
How often I convinced myself, after the march began,
that my stumble in the gateway promised ill!
Let no man dare depart from a reluctant love
or he shall know that God forbade his going.

What help, O Delia, your Queen of Heaven now –
devout percussions of the bronze rattle,
observance of the ritual ablutions,
nights apart so memorably pure?
Haste, Goddess, to my aid, for many a painted tablet
on temple walls proclaims your saving power;
and then my Delia, in payment of her vow,
linen-clad shall sit before your holy door
and twice a day with loosened hair duly tell your praises,
conspicuous among the Egyptian congregation.
But grant that I may worship the Penates of my fathers
and offer incense every month to the ancient Lar.

How good the life in Saturn's reign, before
the world was opened into long roads!
Pine timbers then had not defied blue waves
or spread billowing canvas to the winds.
No roving sailor seeking profit from strange lands
had freighted ship with foreign merchandise.
No mighty bull in those days bore the yoke
or stallion tamely chawed the bit.
Houses had no doors. No stone stood in the fields
to rule the arable with straight edge.

ipsae mella dabant quercus, ultroque ferebant
    obuia securis ubera lactis oues;
non acies, non ira fuit, non bella, nec ensem
    immiti saeuus duxerat arte faber.

Nunc Ioue sub domino caedes et uulnera semper,
    nunc mare, nunc leti mille repente uiae.   50
parce, Pater: timidum non me periuria terrent,
    non dicta in sanctos impia uerba deos.
quod si fatales iam nunc expleuimus annos,
    fac lapis inscriptis stet super ossa notis:
HIC IACET IMMITI CONSVMPTVS MORTE TIBVLLVS
    MESSALLAM TERRA DVM SEQVITVRQVE MARI.

Sed me, quod facilis tenero sum semper amori,
    ipsa Venus campos ducet in Elysios.
hic choreae cantusque uigent, passimque uagantes
    dulce sonant tenui gutture carmen aues;   60
fert casiam non culta seges totosque per agros
    floret odoratis terra benigna rosis:
ac iuuenum series teneris immixta puellis
    ludit, et assidue proelia miscet Amor.
illic est cuicumque rapax Mors uenit amanti,
    et gerit insigni myrtea serta coma.

At scelerata iacet sedes in nocte profunda
    abdita, quam circum flumina nigra sonant:
Tisiphoneque impexa feros pro crinibus angues
    saeuit et huc illuc impia turba fugit;   70
tunc niger in porta serpentum Cerberus ore
    stridet et aeratas excubat ante fores.
illic Iunonem temptare Ixionis ausi
    uersantur celeri noxia membra rota,
porrectusque nouem Tityos per iugera terrae
    assiduas atro uiscere pascit aues.
Tantalus est illic, et circum stagna, sed acrem
    iam iam poturi deserit unda sitim;
et Danai proles, Veneris quod numina laesit,
    in caua Lethaeas dolia portat aquas.   80
illic sit quicumque meos uiolarit amores,
    optarit lentas et mihi militias.

There was honey from the oak, and heavy-uddered ewes
offered milk on meeting carefree countryfolk.
Anger and armies and war were not yet known:
no blacksmith's cruel craft had forged the sword.

But now, in Jove's dominion, it is always wounds & slaughter;
now there is the sea and sudden Death's one thousand roads.
Have mercy on me, Father, for although I am afraid
no perjury or blasphemy justifies the fear.
But if today I have completed my predestined years
let my bones be laid beneath a stone inscribed
HERE LIES TIBULLUS WASTED BY UNTIMELY DEATH
WHILE SERVING WITH MESSALLA ON LAND AND SEA.

My spirit, though, as I have always welcomed tender love,
Venus herself will lead to the Elysian fields.
There songs and dances flourish, and flitting everywhere
sweetly sing the birds their slender-throated tune.
Untilled the land bears cassia and over whole acres
heavy-scented roses bloom from the rich loam.
Young men and tender girls make sport, lined up together,
continually engaging in the battles of Love.
There are all those whom Death raped while they were lovers
and they wear the myrtle in token on their hair.

But the place of wickedness lies hidden deep in night
and all around it black rivers roar.
Tisiphone, the Fury with snakes for hair uncombed,
whips in all directions the godless multitude.
Then, black in the gateway, Cerberus serpent-mouthed
hisses, lying guard before the brazen door.
There the guilty limbs of Juno's would-be ravisher,
the bold Ixion, twist on the whirling wheel.
And Tityos, spreadeagled over nine terrestrial acres,
feeds with bleeding flesh the indefatigable birds.
There in the pool is Tantalus, but when he stoops to drink
the water slides away from his raging thirst.
And the Danaids, who violated Venus' majesty,
are heaving Lethe water into leaking vats.
Let any man lie there who desecrates my love
and prays for my long service in the army.

At tu casta, precor, maneas sanctique pudoris
    assideat custos sedula semper anus.
haec tibi fabellas referat positaque lucerna
    deducat plena stamina longa colu,
ac circa, grauibus pensis affixa, puella
    paulatim somno fessa remittat opus.
tunc ueniam subito nec quisquam nuntiet ante
    sed uidear caelo missus adesse tibi.   90
tunc mihi, qualis eris, longos turbata capillos,
    obuia nudato, Delia, curre pede.
hoc precor; hunc illum nobis Aurora nitentem
    Luciferum roseis candida portet equis.

IV

'Sic umbrosa tibi contingant tecta, Priape,
    ne capiti soles ne noceantque niues:
quae tua formosos cepit sollertia? certe
    non tibi barba nitet, non tibi culta coma est;
nudus et hibernae producis frigora brumae,
    nudus et aestiui tempora sicca Canis.'

Sic ego. tum Bacchi respondit rustica proles,
    armatus curua, sic mihi, falce deus:
'O fuge te tenerae puerorum credere turbae,
    nam causam iusti semper amoris habent.   10
hic placet angustis quod equum compescit habenis;
    hic placidam niueo pectore pellit aquam.
hic quia fortis adest audacia cepit; at illi
    uirgineus teneras stat pudor ante genas.

Sed ne te capiant, primo si forte negabit,
    taedia: paulatim sub iuga colla dabit.
longa dies homini docuit parere leones;
    longa dies molli saxa peredit aqua.
annus in apricis maturat collibus uuas;
    annus agit certa lucida signa uice.   20

Nec iurare time: Veneris periuria uenti
    irrita per terras et freta summa ferunt.
gratia magna Ioui: uetuit pater ipse ualere
    iurasset cupide quicquid ineptus amor;

But, Delia, please be true to me, and let the old duenna
be there to guard your honour with her continual care.
She shall tell you stories and when the lamp is lit
draw the lengthening thread from her laden distaff,
while the girls around her, intent on heavy stints,
gradually for weariness nod off at their work.
Then suddenly I shall arrive and no one give you warning
but your first thought will be that I have dropped from heaven.
Then, simply as you are, in long-haired confusion,
run to greet me, Delia, with naked feet.
That is my desire: let bright Aurora bring me
on her rose-red steeds that shining Morning Star.

4

'So may a shady roof be given you, Priapus,
to protect your person from the sun and snow,
if you tell me your technique for catching handsome boys.
Not yours, I see, the wavy hair, not yours the glossy beard,
and naked you prolong the cold of winter solstice,
naked too the drought of summer Sirius.'

Thus I. Whereat the God armed with a reaping-hook,
Bacchus' yokel son, thus to me replied:
'O flee and never trust thee to the troop of tender boys,
for cause of true love evermore is theirs.
Here is one who pleases by his skill in horsemanship;
there another who can part the pool with pale white breast.
This one's impudence is charming, while on that one's tender cheek
innocence mounts blushing guard.

Yet be thou of good courage if at first he should refuse.
Slowly will he bring his neck beneath the yoke.
Time can teach the lion obedience to man;
gentle water bites through the rock in time.
A year revolves the shining signs in regular succession;
grapes on sunny slopes ripen in a year.

And fear thou not to swear. The perjuries of Venus
are blown invalid over land and sea.
All thanks be to the Father. For Jove himself forbade
the longing oaths of lovers to have weight.

perque suas impune sinit Dictynna sagittas
    affirmes, crines perque Minerua suos.

At si tardus eris errabis. transiet aetas
    quam cito! non segnis stat remeatue dies.
quam cito purpureos deperdit terra colores!
    quam cito formosas populus alta comas!   30
quam iacet, infirmae uenere ubi fata senectae,
    qui prior Eleo est carcere missus equus!
uidi iam iuuenem premeret cum serior aetas
    maerentem stultos praeteriisse dies.
crudeles diui. serpens nouus exuit annos;
    formae non ullam Fata dedere moram.
solis aeterna est Baccho Phoeboque iuuentas,
    nam decet intonsus crinis utrumque deum.

Tu puero quodcumque tuo temptare libebit
    cedas: obsequio plurima uincet amor.   40
neu comes ire neges quamuis uia longa paretur
    et Canis arenti torreat arua siti,
quamuis praetexens picta ferrugine caelum
    uenturam†amiciat† imbrifer arcus aquam.
uel si caeruleas puppi uolet ire per undas,
    ipse leuem remo per freta pelle ratem.
nec te paeniteat duros subiisse labores
    aut opera insuetas atteruisse manus.
nec, uelit insidiis altas si claudere ualles,
    dum placeas, umeri retia ferre negent.   50
si uolet arma, leui temptabis ludere dextra;
    saepe dabis nudum, uincat ut ille, latus.
tunc tibi mitis erit, rapias tum cara licebit
    oscula: pugnabit sed tibi rapta dabit.
rapta dabit primo, post afferet ipse roganti,
    post etiam collo se implicuisse uelit.

Heu male nunc artes miseras haec saecula tractant!
    iam tener assueuit munera uelle puer.
at tu qui Venerem docuisti uendere primus,
    quisquis es, infelix urgeat ossa lapis.   60
Pieridas, pueri, doctos et amate poetas,
    aurea nec superent munera Pieridas.

A promise by Diana's arrows or Minerva's hair
may be broken without fear of punishment.

But wait too long & thou'lt be wrong. How swiftly prime is flying!
Time is never idle, never turns again.
How swiftly disappear earth's lively colours!
How swiftly the tall poplar's lovely locks!
How fall'n, when Fate brings on old age & weakness,
the horse that was Olympic winner once!
A young man have I seen with middle age upon him
lament the foolish passing of his days.
Ah, cruel Gods! The snake re-born sloughs off its years
but Fate has granted Beauty no delaying.
Bacchus & Apollo have sole right to eternal youth,
for long hair suits their twin divinity.

Then humour thou the boy in all he has a mind to:
Love will conquer most by giving in.
Deny him not thy company upon the longest journey,
though the thirsty Dog-star parches the ground,
though bordering the sky with dim & dusky colours
the rainbow warns of an approaching storm.
If he should wish to sail across the billows blue
row the dinghy o'er the main thyself.
And let it not repent thee of thy labour and distress
or of blisters on thine unaccustomed hands.
Should he then desire to set a snare in some high valley
shoulder thou the nets, if haply thou canst please.
Or if he fancy fencing fence thou not with heavy hand;
oft expose thy flank and suffer him to win.
Then will he be kind to thee – thou'lt steal a precious kiss.
He will surely struggle, but grant thee kisses stolen.
Stolen kisses first, thereafter kisses for the asking,
then will he peradventure embrace thee on his own.

Alas, an evil generation treateth not the Arts aright:
tender boys are now accustomed to seek gifts.
Woe to him who first taught the marketing of Venus!
Let the stone of stumbling lie upon his bones.
Love the Muses, O ye striplings, & the scholar poets,
nor above the Muses value gifts of gold.

carmine purpurea est Nisi coma; carmina ni sint,
  ex umero Pelopis non nituisset ebur.
quem referent Musae uiuet dum robora tellus,
  dum caelum stellas, dum uehet amnis aquas.
at qui non audit Musas, qui uendit amorem,
  Idaeae currus ille sequatur Opis
et ter centenas erroribus expleat urbes
  et secet ad Phrygios uilia membra modos.   70
blanditiis uult esse locum Venus: illa querelis
  supplicibus, miseris fletibus illa fauet.'

Haec mihi quae canerem Titio deus edidit ore,
  sed Titium coniunx haec meminisse uetat.
pareat ille suae: uos me celebrate magistrum
  quos male habet multa callidus arte puer.
gloria cuique sua est: me qui spernentur amantes
  consultent; cunctis ianua nostra patet.
tempus erit cum me Veneris praecepta ferentem
  deducat iuuenum sedula turba senem.   80

Eheu, quam Marathus lento me torquet amore!
  deficiunt artes deficiuntque doli.
parce, puer, quaeso – ne turpis fabula fiam
  cum mea ridebunt uana magisteria.

                    V

Asper eram et bene discidium me ferre loquebar,
  at mihi nunc longe gloria fortis abest;
namque agor, ut per plana citus sola uerbere turben
  quem celer assueta uersat ab arte puer.
ure ferum et torque, libeat ne dicere quicquam
  magnificum posthac: horrida uerba doma.
parce tamen, per te furtiui foedera lecti,
  per Venerem quaeso compositumque caput.

Ille ego, cum tristi morbo defessa iaceres,
  te dicor uotis eripuisse meis.   10
ipseque te circum lustraui sulpure puro,
  carmine cum magico praecinuisset anus.
ipse procuraui ne possent saeua nocere
  somnia ter sancta deueneranda mola.

Nisus' lock in song is purple; were it not for song
never had the ivory shone from Pelops' shoulder.
He of whom the Muses tell shall live while earth bears oak-trees
and the heaven stars and the rivers water.
But he who hears the Muses not, who makes of love a market,
shall follow the Idaean chariot of Ops
and traversing three hundred cities in his wanderings
cut off his vile members to the Phrygian mode.
Venus wills a place for lovingkindness & she hears
the suppliant's complaint & the tears of the afflicted.'

To this, my song for Titius, the God gave utterance,
but Titius' wife commands him to forget it.
Let him obey his own. But let all you who suffer
the wiles of crafty boys hail me as Master.
To each his own ambition. Mine is counselling rejected
lovers. Yes, my door stands open to them all.
The time will come when I as bearer of Love's message
am attended in old age by troops of studious youth.

Alas, how Marathus in love's slow fire torments me!
Science profits nothing – neither do arts.
Have pity, boy, I beg you, or my reputation's gone
and all will ridicule the magisterial fool.

                5

I was angry & proclaimed that separation did not hurt,
but such heroics now are far beyond me.
I am driven, like a top spinning on a flat surface,
whipped by an agile boy who knows his business.
Twist & sear my pride with torture till I never fancy
grandiloquence again. Tame my ranting speech.
But forgive me, I beseech you, by the bond of stolen love,
by Venus & the heads of our agreement.

When you lay exhausted on the bed of fever,
mine, I am assured, were the prayers that saved you.
It was I who purified your room with burning sulphur
after the wise woman had chanted her spells;
I who counteracted the menace of your nightmares,
offering holy meal thrice in expiation;

ipse ego, uelatus filo tunicisque solutis,
    uota nouem Triuiae nocte silente dedi.
omnia persolui: fruitur nunc alter amore,
    et precibus felix utitur ille meis.

At mihi felicem uitam, si salua fuisses,
    fingebam demens, sed renuente deo: 20
'rura colam, frugumque aderit mea Delia custos,
    area dum messes sole calente teret;
aut mihi seruabit plenis in lintribus uuas
    pressaque ueloci candida musta pede.
consuescet numerare pecus; consuescet amantis
    garrulus in dominae ludere uerna sinu.
illa deo sciet agricolae pro uitibus uuam,
    pro segete spicas, pro grege ferre dapem.
illa regat cunctos, illi sint omnia curae,
    ac iuuet in tota me nihil esse domo.   30
huc ueniet Messalla meus, cui dulcia poma
    Delia selectis detrahat arboribus,
et tantum uenerata uirum, hunc sedula curet,
    huic paret atque epulas ipsa ministra gerat.'

Haec mihi fingebam, quae nunc Caurusque Notusque
    iactat odoratos uota per Armenios.
saepe ego temptaui curas depellere uino:
    at dolor in lacrimas uerterat omne merum.
saepe aliam tenui: sed iam cum gaudia adirem
    admonuit dominae deseruitque Venus.   40
tunc me, discedens, deuotum femina dixit –
    a pudet! – et narrat scire nefanda meam.
non facit hoc uerbis; facie tenerisque lacertis
    deuouet et flauis nostra puella comis.
talis ad Haemonium Nereis Pelea quondam
    uecta est frenato caerula pisce Thetis.

Haec nocuere mihi: quod adest nunc diues amator,
    uenit in exitium callida lena meum.
sanguineas edat illa dapes atque ore cruento
    tristia cum multo pocula felle bibat.   50
hanc uolitent animae circum sua fata querentes
    semper et e tectis strix uiolenta canat.

44

I who wearing woollen fillet & unbelted tunic
in the silent night made nine vows to Diana.
I paid them all, and now someone else enjoys my love
and profits from my prayers, the lucky man.

In my folly I had dreamed that the lucky life was mine
if you recovered, but the God willed otherwise.
'I'll farm' I thought '& Delia will be there to guard the grain
while the sun-baked floor threshes harvest in the heat.
Or she will watch the grapes for me in the laden troughs
& the white new wine pressed by trampling feet.
She will learn to count the sheep. The children of the house-slaves
will learn to play & prattle on a loving mistress' lap.
She will offer to the farmer God grapes for the vines,
ears for the standing corn, a victim for the flock.
She can rule us all, take charge of everything,
and I'll enjoy non-entity at home.
When my Messalla comes to see us, Delia will pick him
delicious apples from our choicest trees,
and in the great man's honour attend to all his needs,
prepare a dinner for him & wait on him herself.'

These were my dreams of happiness but now south-western breezes
toss them unfulfilled beyond perfumed Armenia.
Often have I tried to drink away my troubles,
but the sorrow turned every wine to tears;
often embraced another, but Venus on joy's brink
reminding me of Delia forsook me.
Then calling me bewitched the woman left & to my shame
spread rumours that my girl uses the black arts.
What need has she of spells, with that bewitching face,
soft arms and yellow hair
like the Nereid of old who rode a bridled dolphin
to Thessalian Peleus – Thetis the blue-eyed?

Such my downfall. Now, a crafty bawd plans my destruction,
having introduced a wealthy lover.
Let her eat raw meat and her lips drip blood
as she drinks full cups of bitter gall.
Let the ghosts flap round her bewailing their fate
and the vampire-owl screech from her eaves.

ipsa fame stimulante furens herbasque sepulcris
    quaerat et a saeuis ossa relicta lupis;
currat et inguinibus nudis ululetque per urbem,
    post agat e triuiis aspera turba canum.
eueniet: dat signa deus. sunt numina amanti,
    saeuit et iniusta lege relicta Venus.

At tu quam primum sagae praecepta rapacis
    desere. num donis uincitur omnis amor?   60
pauper erit praesto semper tibi, pauper adibit
    primus et in tenero fixus erit latere.
pauper in angusto fidus comes agmine turbae
    subicietque manus efficietque uiam.
pauper ad occultos furtim deducet amicos
    uinclaque de niueo detrahet ipse pede.

Heu, canimus frustra, nec uerbis uicta patescit
    ianua, sed plena est percutienda manu.
at tu, qui potior nunc es, mea fata timeto:
    uersatur celeri fors leuis orbe rotae.   70
non frustra quidam iam nunc in limine perstat
    sedulus, ac crebro prospicit, ac refugit,
et simulat transire domum, mox deinde recurrit
    solus, et ante ipsas exscreat usque fores.
nescioquid furtiuus Amor parat. utere, quaeso,
    dum licet: in liquida nat tibi linter aqua.

                VI

Semper, ut inducar, blandos offers mihi uultus,
    post tamen es misero tristis et asper, Amor.
quid tibi saeuitiae mecum est! an gloria magna est
    insidias homini composuisse deum?

Nam mihi tenduntur casses. iam Delia furtim
    nescioquem tacita callida nocte fouet.
illa quidem tam multa negat, sed credere durum est;
    sic etiam de me pernegat usque uiro.
ipse miser docui quo posset ludere pacto
    custodes: eheu, nunc premor arte mea.   10
fingere tunc didicit causas ut sola cubaret,
    cardine tunc tacito uertere posse fores.

Let her go hunger-mad and search for herbs on graves,
for any bone left over by ravening wolves.
Let her run with naked crotch, howling through the city,
hunted by a savage pack of crossroad curs.
So be it. God has given the sign. A power stands over lovers
and Venus takes revenge when unlawfully abandoned.

O Delia reject forthwith that grasping witch's guidance.
Must every love surrender to a bribe?
Your poor man is prepared to offer service always,
the first to come at need, inseparate from your side.
Your poor man, trusty comrade in the pressure of a crowd,
will use his hands to good effect & find a way.
Your poor man will escort you unobserved to secret friends,
slipping the sandal from your snow-white foot himself.

Alas I sing in vain. Her door unmoved by words
is waiting for the knock of a money-laden hand.
But you, her darling of today, take warning from my fate.
Fortune's fickle wheel quickly turns.
Not for nothing even now someone stands upon her threshold –
first he looks about him, then he backs away,
and pretends to pass the house, then returns without his slave
and coughs persistently right by the door.
Love the thief has plans. Take your pleasure while you may.
Water is unstable and your ship is still at sea.

6

Always, to entice me, Love, you wear a smiling face,
but later to my sorrow assume an angry frown.
How hard on me you are! Is it so glorious
for an immortal God to set a man-trap?

Your nets are spread against me, now that devious Delia
in the secrecy of night hugs another man.
True, she denies it strongly, but belief is difficult;
she makes the same denials to her husband about me.
It was I, alas, who taught her how to fool the guard,
and now I am the victim of my own device.
She learnt to find excuses then for sleeping on her own,
to open creaking doors without a sound

tunc sucos herbasque dedi quis liuor abiret
  quem facit impresso mutua dente Venus.

At tu, fallacis coniunx incaute puellae,
  me quoque seruato peccet ut illa nihil.
neu iuuenes celebret multo sermone caueto,
  neue cubet laxo pectus aperta sinu,
neu te decipiat nutu, digitoque liquorem
  ne trahat et mensae ducat in orbe notas.   20
exibit cum saepe, time, seu uisere dicet
  sacra Bonae maribus non adeunda Deae.
at mihi si credas, illam sequar unus ad aras;
  tunc mihi non oculis sit timuisse meis.

Saepe, uelut gemmas eius signumque probarem,
  per causam memini me tetigisse manum.
saepe mero somnum peperi tibi, at ipse bibebam
  sobria supposita pocula uictor aqua.
non ego te laesi prudens; ignosce fatenti.
  iussit Amor: contra quis ferat arma deos?   30
ille ego sum (nec me iam dicere uera pudebit)
  instabat tota cui tua nocte canis.
quid tenera tibi coniuge opus? tua si bona nescis
  seruare, frustra clauis inest foribus.
te tenet, absentes alios suspirat amores
  et simulat subito condoluisse caput.

At mihi seruandam credas: non saeua recuso
  uerbera, detrecto non ego uincla pedum.
tunc procul absitis, quisquis colit arte capillos,
  et fluit effuso cui toga laxa sinu;   40
quisquis et occurret, ne possit crimen habere
  stet procul aut alia *transeat ille* uia.

Sic fieri iubet ipse deus, sic magna sacerdos
  est mihi diuino uaticinata sono.
haec, ubi Bellonae motu est agitata, nec acrem
  flammam, non amens uerbera torta timet.
ipsa bipenne suos caedit uiolenta lacertos
  sanguineque effuso spargit inulta deam,
statque latus praefixa ueru, stat saucia pectus,
  et canit euentus quos dea magna monet: 50

and use the herbs and simples that I gave her to remove
the marks imprinted by the teeth of passion.

But you, sir, careless husband of a deceitful girl,
keep watch on both of us to stop her playing false.
Take care she does not talk too much with young admirers
or at a dinner wear a dress that shows her breast
or fool you with a nod or dip her finger in the wine
and trace a secret message on the table-top.
Worry when she's often out or tells you she'll attend
the rites of the Good Goddess, where men are not allowed.
If you trusted her to me, she'd attend with my attendance
and as the one man present I'd not fear for my eyes.

Often I remember how I touched her hand
on pretext of appraising her signet cameo,
& how my wine sent you to sleep while I drank sober cups
victoriously substituting water.
The sin was not cold-blooded & confession earns forgiveness.
It was Love that gave the order. Who can fight against a God?
I was the man – no longer shall I blush to tell the truth –
the man your dog was barking at that night.
What good's a tender wife to you? If you can't keep your treasure
locked doors are little use.
Her sighs while she embraces you are for an absent lover
and the sudden head-ache is a subterfuge.

But let *me* be her keeper. You could flog me when you liked
or fling me into fetters & I'd take my punishment.
Then they'd have to clear off, all those fops with curly hair
and expansive togas falling in loose folds.
Anyone who met us would be halted at a distance
or pass us by another road to prove his innocence.

Thus runs the God's commandment, this Bellona's high-priestess
with utterance inspired prophesied to me.
When in trance, possessed & shaken by the goddess,
she fears no roaring flame or flailing scourge,
slashes her own arms in frenzy with a double axe,
unscathed soaks the image in a stream of blood,
& standing there with wounded breast & skewered flank
chants Bellona's warning oracles:

'parcite quam custodit Amor uiolare puellam,
    ne pigeat magno post tetigisse malo.
attigerit, labentur opes, ut uulnere nostro
    sanguis, ut hic uentis diripiturque cinis.'

Et tibi nescioquam dixit, mea Delia, poenam;
    si tamen admittas, sit precor illa leuis.
non ego te propter parco tibi, sed tua mater
    me mouet atque iras aurea uincit anus.
haec mihi te adducit tenebris multioque timore
    coniungit nostras clam taciturna manus.   60
haec foribusque manet noctu me affixa proculque
    cognoscit strepitus me ueniente pedum.

Viue diu mihi, dulcis anus: proprios ego tecum,
    sit modo fas, annos contribuisse uelim.
te semper natamque tuam te propter amabo:
    quicquid agit, sanguis est tamen illa tuus.
sit modo casta doce, quamuis non uitta ligatos
    impediat crines nec stola longa pedes.
et mihi sint durae leges, laudare nec ullam
    possim ego quin oculos appetat illa meos;   70
et, siquid peccasse putet, ducarque capillis
    immerito pronas proripiarque uias.

Non ego te pulsare uelim, sed uenerit iste
    si furor, optarim non habuisse manus.
nec saeuo sis casta metu sed mente fideli;
    mutuus absenti te mihi seruet amor.
at quae fida fuit nulli, post uicta senecta
    ducit inops tremula stamina torta manu,
firmaque conductis adnectit licia telis,
    tractaque de niueo uellere ducta putat.   80
hanc animo gaudente uident iuuenumque cateruae
    commemorant merito tot mala ferre senem.
hanc Venus ex alto flentem sublimis Olympo
    spectat et infidis quam sit acerba monet.

Haec aliis maledicta cadant. nos, Delia, amoris
    exemplum cana simus uterque coma.

'See ye do no violence to the girl whom Love protects,
lest ye repent of touching her to your great evil after.
If any man should touch her his wealth shall flow away
as blood flows from my wounds & wind scatters this ash.'

She also spoke of punishment for you, my Delia,
but if you should transgress I pray it may be light.
I spare you for your mother's sake & not your own deserving;
old & golden-hearted she disarms my wrath.
In the dark she leads you to me & though terrified
stealthily with no word spoken joins our hands.
Pressed to the door at night, she listens, waiting for me –
can recognise, far off, approaching steps as mine.

Long life to you, sweet lady. If it were possible
I'd give you part of mine.
You I shall always love & thanks to you your daughter;
she is still your blood however she behaves.
But teach her to be faithful though her braided hair is free
& no Roman wife's long robe confines her feet.
I too can take harsh terms: if I praise another woman
Delia is welcome to attack my eyes;
& if she thinks me false she can pull me by the hair
& drag me in my innocence along the street face down.

I'd never strike you, Delia, but should the mad fit come
I'd pray to lose my hands.
Be true then not from fear but faithfulness of heart.
Let mutual love for me in absence guard you.
The woman true to no one, when overcome by age
must pull the yarn with shaking hand, a pauper,
& tie the leashes firm to a hired loom & clean
the locks of wool pulled out from snow-white fleeces.
Her plight gives hearty pleasure to all the young men watching,
who declare it serves her right to suffer in old age.
Aloof on high Olympus Venus sees her tears & warns us
how merciless she is to infidelity.

But these ill wishes are for others. Delia, you & I
must be Love's paradigm when we are both white-haired.

VII

Hunc cecinere diem Parcae, fatalia nentes
    stamina non ulli dissoluenda deo:
hunc fore Aquitanas posset qui fundere gentes,
    quem tremeret forti milite uictus Atur.
euenere: nouos pubes Romana triumphos
    uidit et euinctos bracchia capta duces;
at te uictrices lauros, Messalla, gerentem
    portabat nitidis currus eburnus equis.

Non sine me est tibi partus honos: Tarbella Pyrene
    testis et Oceani litora Santonici,   10
testis Arar Rhodanusque celer magnusque Garunna,
    Carnutis et flaui caerula lympha Liger.

An te, Cydne, canam, tacitis qui leniter undis
    caeruleus placidae per uada serpis aquae?
quantus et aetherio contingens uertice nubes
    frigidus intonsos Taurus alat Cilicas?
quid referam ut uolitet crebras intacta per urbes
    alba Palaestino sancta columba Syro?
utque maris uastum prospectet turribus aequor
    prima ratem uentis credere docta Tyros?   20
qualis et, arentes cum findit Sirius agros,
    fertilis aestiua Nilus abundet aqua?

Nile pater, quanam possim te dicere causa
    aut quibus in terris occuluisse caput?
te propter nullos tellus tua postulat imbres,
    arida nec pluuio supplicat herba Ioui.
te canit utque suum pubes miratur Osirim
    barbara, Memphitem plangere docta bouem.

Primus aratra manu sollerti fecit Osiris
    et teneram ferro sollicitauit humum.   30
primus inexpertae commisit semina terrae
    pomaque non notis legit ab arboribus.
hic docuit teneram palis adiungere uitem,
    hic uiridem dura caedere falce comam.
illi iucundos primum matura sapores
    expressa incultis uua dedit pedibus.

7

Of this day sang the Fates, as they spun the threads of doom
that no God can unwind:
this would be the day of rout for tribes of Aquitaine,
of dread for the Adour, conquered by brave cohorts.
And so it came to pass. Our Roman race has seen
new Triumphs, chiefs with captive wrists in chains,
and you, Messalla, wearing the victorious laurel,
drawn by shining steeds in the ivory chariot.

Not without me was your glory gained: witness the Tarbellian
Pyrenees and shores of the Santonic Ocean;
witness Saône and rapid Rhone and great Garonne
and Loire, blue stream of flaxen-haired Carnutes.

Or shall I sing of Cydnus, whose quiet waters glide
softly through smooth blue shallows?
Of Taurus, cold & huge, with airy summit cloudcapped,
unshorn Cilicia's livelihood?
Why tell of white doves flying, safe through crowded towns,
sacrosanct in Syropalestine?
How the tall towers of Tyre, the mother of sailing ships,
survey the sea's expanse?
How fertile Nile floods in summer
when Sirius cracks the thirsty fields?

Where or wherefore, Father Nile,
can I say you hide your head?
Thanks to you your country never prays for rain;
no withered grass petitions pluvial Jupiter.
Your folk in barbarous lamentation for the Memphian bull
praise & worship you as their Osiris.

The skilled hands of Osiris constructed the first plough,
solicited the virgin soil with iron,
committed the first seed to inexperienced earth
& gathered fruit from unfamiliar trees.
Osiris taught the tying of the tender vine to poles,
the lopping of green hair with pruning-hooks.
To him the ripe grapes trodden by uncultivated feet
first gave delicious savours.

ille liquor docuit uoces inflectere cantu,
    mouit et ad certos nescia membra modos.
Bacchus et agricolae magno confecta labore
    pectora laetitiae dissoluenda dedit.   40
Bacchus et afflictis requiem mortalibus affert,
    crura licet dura compede pulsa sonent.
non tibi sunt tristes curae nec luctus, Osiri,
    sed chorus et cantus et leuis aptus amor,
sed uarii flores et frons redimita corymbis,
    fusa sed ad teneros lutea palla pedes,
et Tyriae uestes et dulcis tibia cantu
    et leuis occultis conscia cista sacris.

Huc ades et Genium ludis Geniumque choreis
    concelebra et multo tempora funde mero.   50
illius et nitido stillent unguenta capillo,
    et capite et collo mollia serta gerat.
sic uenias, hodierne: tibi dem turis honores,
    liba et Mopsopio dulcia melle feram.

At tibi succrescat proles quae facta parentis
    augeat et circa stet ueneranda senem.
nec taceat monumenta uiae quem Tuscula tellus
    candidaque antiquo detinet Alba Lare.
namque opibus congesta tuis, hic glarea dura
    sternitur, hic apta iungitur arte silex.   60
te canat agricola a magna cum uenerit Vrbe
    serus inoffensum rettuleritque pedem.

At tu, Natalis, multos celebrande per annos,
    candidior semper candidiorque ueni.

VIII

Non ego celari possum quid nutus amantis
    quidue ferant miti lenia uerba sono,
nec mihi sunt sortes nec conscia fibra deorum,
    praecinit euentus nec mihi cantus auis:
ipsa Venus magico religatum bracchia nodo
    perdocuit, multis non sine uerberibus.
desine dissimulare: deus crudelius urit
    quos uidet inuitos succubuisse sibi.

That liquor taught the modulations of the voice in song,
moving ignorant limbs to sure rhythms.
To farmers' hearts exhausted by long labour
Bacchus brings deliverance & joy.
Bacchus offers respite to mortals in affliction,
though chains clank on their ankles.
Not sorrow or dull care, but song & dance, Osiris,
& fickle love suit you,
& flowers of every colour, brows with ivy-berries bound,
robes of saffron flowing down to tender feet,
Tyrian fabrics, dulcet melodies upon the pipe,
& the wicker casket for your holy mysteries.

O hither come & join us in the games & in the dances
to celebrate the Genius & drench his brow with wine.
Let perfumes of anointing drip from his gleaming locks
& garlands soft adorn his head & neck.
So come you, hodiernal: I will honour you with incense
& bring you meal-cake sweetened with the honey of Hymettus.

Messalla, may your family grow up to increase your glory
& stand about you in old age with honour.
May visitors to Tusculum & white Alba's ancient Lar
talk of your memorial, the road –
for here is hard-packed gravel laid at your expense
& here are stone blocks fitted skilfully together.
May farmers sing of you, as they come from the great city,
returning in the dark without a stumble.

And may your Birthday Spirit attend his celebration
bright & ever brighter for many years to come.

8

I cannot miss the augury of a lover's nod
or gently whispered words,
and yet I use no lots or divinatory lobes
and hear no prophecy in bird-song.
Venus herself, tying my arms with magic knot,
has flogged me to full knowledge.
Be honest, then. The God has fiercer fires
for those unwilling to submit to him.

Quid tibi nunc molles prodest coluisse capillos
    saepeque mutatas disposuisse comas?
quid fuco splendente genas ornare? quid ungues
    artificis docta subsecuisse manu?
frustra iam uestes, frustra mutantur amictus
    ansaque compressos colligat arta pedes.
illa placet, quamuis inculto uenerit ore
    nec nitidum tarda compserit arte caput.

Num te carminibus, num te pallentibus herbis
    deuouit tacito tempore noctis anus?
cantus uicinis fruges traducit ab agris,
    cantus et iratae detinet anguis iter,
cantus et e curru Lunam deducere temptat,
    et faceret si non aera repulsa sonent.

Quid queror, heu, misero carmen nocuisse? quid herbas?
    forma nihil magicis utitur auxiliis,
sed corpus tetigisse nocet, sed longa dedisse
    oscula, sed femori conseruisse femur.

Nec tu difficilis puero tamen esse memento;
    persequitur poenis tristia facta Venus.
munera nec poscas; det munera canus amator
    ut foueat molli frigida membra sinu.
carior est auro iuuenis cui leuia fulgent
    ora nec amplexus aspera barba terit.
huic tu candentes umero suppone lacertos
    et regum magnae despiciantur opes.

At Venus inuenit puero concumbere furtim,
    dum timet, et teneros conserere usque sinus,
et dare anhelanti pugnantibus umida linguis
    oscula et in collo figere dente notas.

Non lapis hanc gemmaeque iuuant quae frigore sola
    dormiat et nulli sit cupienda uiro.
heu sero reuocatur amor seroque iuuentas
    cum uetus infecit cana senecta caput.
tum studium formae est; coma tum mutatur ut annos
    dissimulet uiridi cortice tincta nucis;

It does you no good now to cultivate those curls
and try out various hair-styles,
no good to paint your cheeks with bright orchella
and have your nails professionally trimmed.
It's useless to keep changing your tunic & your cloak
& cramp your feet in tight-laced shoes.
You love that girl, although she wears no make-up
& takes no pains to sleek her hair.

Maybe some beldame in the silent night
with spells or pallid herbs bewitched you?
Spells can lift the crops from neighbours' fields,
can halt the hissing snake,
would draw the Moon down from her chariot
if brasses were not clashed.

Alas why blame the poor boy's hurt on spells or herbs?
Beauty needs no magic aids.
What hurts is body's touch, and giving long kisses,
and pressing thigh to thigh.

So, Pholoe, remember to take him seriously,
albeit but a boy. Venus punishes unkindness.
Demand no gifts, but make your grizzled gallant give
to warm his chilly limbs in soft embrace.
Dearer than gold the youth with smooth & shining face
whose kiss no stubble rasps.
Under this one's shoulder lay your dazzling arms
and look down on the wealth of kings.

Venus found the way to lie with a timid lad
by stealth, to join embrace in close encounter,
to give moist kisses, breathless in the duel of tongues,
and bite her cipher on his neck.

No pearl or precious stone can pleasure her who sleeps
in the cold alone, no man's desire.
Too late alas is love and too late youth recalled
when white-haired age has stained the head.
Beauty then is studied. Hair is changed to hide
the years with dye from a nut's green rind.

tollere tum cura est albos a stirpe capillos
    et faciem dempta pelle referre nouam.

At tu, dum primi floret tibi temporis aetas,
    utere: non tardo labitur illa pede.
neu Marathum torque. puero quae gloria uicto est?
    in ueteres esto dura, puella, senes.   50
parce, precor, tenero. non illi sontica causa est,
    sed nimius luto corpora tingit amor.

Heu miser absenti maestas quam saepe querelas
    conicit, et lacrimis omnia plena madent.
'quid me spernis?' ait. 'poterat custodia uinci;
    ipse dedit cupidis fallere posse deus.
nota Venus furtiua mihi est – ut lenis agatur
    spiritus, ut nec dent oscula rapta sonum.
et possum media quouis obrepere nocte
    et strepitu nullo clam reserare fores.   60
quid prosunt artes, miserum si spernit amantem
    et fugit ex ipso saeua puella toro?
uel cum promittit subito sed perfida fallit
    et mihi nox multis est uigilanda malis?
dum mihi uenturam fingo, quodcumque mouetur
    illius credo tunc sonuisse pedes.'

Desistas lacrimare, puer. non frangitur illa,
    et tua iam fletu lumina fessa tument.
oderunt, Pholoe, moneo, fastidia diui,
    nec prodest sanctis tura dedisse focis.   70
hic Marathus quondam miseros ludebat amantes,
    nescius ultorem post caput esse deum.
saepe etiam lacrimas fertur risisse dolentis
    et cupidum ficta detinuisse mora.
nunc omnes odit fastus, nunc displicet illi
    quaecumque opposita est ianua dura sera.
et te poena manet, ni desinis esse superba.
    quam cupies uotis hunc reuocare diem!

IX

Quid mihi, si fueras miseros laesurus amores,
    foedera per diuos clam uiolanda dabas?

58

Solicitude then turns to rooting out white hairs
and recovers face by slack skin's removal.

Therefore while there flowers for you the season of the prime
use it, for it slips away fleet-footed.
And do not torture Marathus. What glory in a boy's defeat?
Be hard in girlhood on your veterans
but spare the innocent. No need to isolate his sickness.
That pallor is a symptom of immoderate love.

Alas, poor lad, how often he reproaches you in absence
and floods the place with tears!
'Why do you scorn me?' he asks. 'The guard could be won over.
God himself gives lovers licence to deceive.
I know clandestine Venus – how to draw breath gently
and steal a silent kiss.
I too can creep at midnight anywhere you please
and open doors without a sound.
But what's the good of arts if the cruel girl disdains
her wretched lover, runs away from bed,
and without warning treacherously breaks her word
and I must wake in night-long misery,
imagining that she will come at last
and thinking every movement is her footfall?'

Stop crying, lad. The girl is unrelenting,
and now your tired eyes are swollen with tears.
I warn you, Pholoe: the Gods hate arrogance.
You waste your incense on their altars.
Our Marathus made fools of his poor lovers once,
blind to the avenging God behind him.
They even say he ridiculed their tears of anguish
and kept desire on edge with false excuses.
But now he hates all pride and fails to appreciate
the opposition of a bolted door.
You too will pay the price unless you stop being proud –
with prayers of yearning for today's return.

9

Why give me solemn promises if you intended wronging
my wretched love by breaking them in secret?

a miser, etsi quis primo periuria celat,
    sera tamen tacitis Poena uenit pedibus.

Parcite, caelestes: aequum est impune licere
    numina formosis laedere uestra semel.
lucra petens habili tauros adiungit aratro
    et durum terrae rusticus urget opus.
lucra petituras freta per parentia uentis
    ducunt instabiles sidera certa rates.
muneribus meus est captus puer: at deus illa
    in cinerem et liquidas munera uertat aquas.
iam mihi persoluet poenas, puluisque decorem
    detrahet et uentis horrida facta coma.
uretur facies, urentur sole capilli,
    deteret inualidos et uia longa pedes.

Admonui quotiens 'auro ne pollue formam:
    saepe solent auro multa subesse mala.
diuitiis captus si quis uiolauit amorem,
    asperaque est illi difficilisque Venus.
ure meum potius flamma caput et pete ferro
    corpus et intorto uerbere terga seca.
nec tibi celandi spes sit peccare paranti:
    scit deus occultos qui uetat esse dolos.
ipse deus tacito permisit saepe ministro
    ederet ut multo libera uerba mero.
ipse deus somno domitos emittere uocem
    iussit et inuitos facta tegenda loqui.'

Haec ego dicebam: nunc me fleuisse loquentem,
    nunc pudet ad teneros procubuisse pedes.
tunc mihi iurabas nullo te diuitis auri
    pondere, non gemmis uendere uelle fidem,
non tibi si pretium Campania terra daretur,
    non tibi si Bacchi cura Falernus ager.
illis eriperes uerbis mihi sidera caeli
    lucere et pronas fluminis esse uias.
quin etiam flebas, at non ego fallere doctus
    tergebam umentes credulus usque genas.
quid faciam, nisi et ipse fores in amore puellae?
    sic precor: exemplo sit leuis illa tuo.

Unhappy boy! Though perjury can be hidden for a time,
punishment is bound to catch you in the end.

Forgive him, Heavenly Powers. Beauty has a right
to wrong your godheads once & go unpunished.
For profit peasants yoke their bulls to the wieldy plough
& press their hard work forward on the land.
For profit, over waters obedient to the winds,
unstable ships are drawn by fixed stars.
My boy was caught by bribery. May God convert those bribes
to ash & running water.
Later he will pay me the punishment in full:
dust & wind-blown hair will slight his charm;
the sun will burn his beauty, bleach his locks;
the long road chafe those vulnerable feet.

'Don't' I often warned him 'don't pollute your bloom with gold.
Behind the gold are sufferings in plenty.
If anyone for money does violence to love,
Venus is hard on him, & difficult.
I'd sooner have my hair burnt off, my body stabbed.
my shoulders lashed with knotted thongs.
But if you plan deception, never hope to hide it;
the God who brings deceit to light – he knows.
The God himself has often authorised free speech
for silent servants in their cups,
has bidden sleepers talk & tell unconsciously
of their most secret deeds.'

Such my advice, but now it shames me to remember
that as I spoke I wept & fell down at your feet.
Then you'd swear to me once more that you'd never sell your promise,
not for pearls & not for pounds of gold,
not for an estate in rich Campania,
not for the Falernian acres Bacchus loves.
Those words could well have robbed me of my certainty
that rivers run downhill & stars shine in the sky.
Yes, you even wept, and I, unschooled in guile,
trusted you & wiped away the tears.
What *should* I do if you were not in love yourself?
May Pholoe be faithless – in your fashion.

O quotiens, uerbis ne quisquam conscius esset,
    ipse comes multa lumina nocte tuli!
saepe insperanti uenit tibi munere nostro
    et latuit clausas post adoperta fores.
tum miser interii, stulte confisus amari;
    nam poteram ad laqueos cautior esse tuos.
quin etiam attonita laudes tibi mente canebam!
    ei mihi, nunc nostri Pieridumque pudet.
illa uelim rapida Vulcanus carmina flamma
    torreat et liquida deleat amnis aqua.   50
tu procul hinc absis, cui formam uendere cura est
    et pretium plena grande referre manu.

At te, qui puerum donis corrumpere es ausus,
    rideat assiduis uxor inulta dolis,
et cum furtiuo iuuenem lassauerit usu,
    tecum interposita languida ueste cubet.
semper sint externa tuo uestigia lecto
    et pateat cupidis semper aperta domus.
nec lasciua soror dicatur plura bibisse
    pocula uel plures emeruisse uiros.   60
illam saepe ferunt conuiuia ducere Baccho
    dum rota Luciferi prouocet orta diem.
illa nulla queat melius consumere noctem
    aut operum uarias disposuisse uices.

At tua perdidicit, nec tu, stultissime, sentis
    cum tibi non solita corpus ab arte mouet.
tune putas illam pro te disponere crines
    aut tenues denso pectere dente comas?
istane persuadet facies auroque lacertos
    uinciat et Tyrio prodeat apta sinu?   70
non tibi sed iuueni cuidam uult bella uideri,
    deuoueat pro quo remque domumque tuam.
nec facit hoc uitio, sed corpora foeda podagra
    et senis amplexus culta puella fugit.

Huic tamen accubuit noster puer! illum ego credam
    cum trucibus Venerem iungere posse feris.
blanditiasne meas aliis tu uendere es ausus?
    tune aliis, demens, oscula ferre mea?

How many times I carried the torch as your attendant
lest any overhear you both conversing,
& paid her money to appear when you despaired of her
or hide outside the door as a surprise!
That was my undoing. Poor fool, I thought you loved me.
I should have been more wary of your snares.
I even versified your praises, moonstruck as I was.
Alas, we & the Muses – how embarrassing!
Let Vulcan roast those eulogies in roaring flame
and the running river liquidate them.
Out of my sight! You only love to sell your looks
& carry home, full-fisted, a fat fee.

But as for you who dared corrupt my boy with bribes,
may your own wife gull you with her cuckoldry
& when her furtive needs have tired out a young lover,
limply lie with you, tunic interposed.
Ever may your bed bear the marks of strangers
& your door be open to the lecherous.
Never be it said that even your licentious sister
sank more wine or served more lovers than your wife.
They tell me that the drinking at her parties often lasts
till Lucifer's bright wheel rolls in the day.
There's no one who can better *spend* the night than she
or play a more exotic range of parts.

Except your wife – she's learnt it all. But you, big fool, don't notice
when she moves her body for you with a new-found ease.
Do you suppose it is for you she sets those curls
or runs the fine comb through that silky hair?
Is yours the face that tempts her to sport the golden bracelets
& leave the house attired in Tyrian gown?
She wants to look attractive for a young man I could name:
for him she'd blast your home & blue your money.
And nobody can blame her. As a girl of taste she finds
your gout & senile gallantry repulsive.

To think my boy has bedded with this creature!
He's capable of coupling with wild beasts.
How could you sell my tendernesses to another man?
How export my kisses? You must be out of your mind.

tunc flebis cum me uinctum puer alter habebit
    et geret in regno regna superba tuo.
at tua tum me poena iuuet, Venerique merenti
    fixa notet casus aurea palma meos:
HANC TIBI FALLACI RESOLVTVS AMORE TIBVLLVS
    DEDICAT ET GRATA SIS DEA MENTE ROGAT.

      X

Quis fuit horrendos primus qui protulit enses?
    quam ferus, et uere ferreus, ille fuit!
tum caedes hominum generi, tum proelia nata;
    tum breuior dirae mortis aperta uia est.

An nihil ille miser meruit, nos ad mala nostra
    uertimus in saeuas quod dedit ille feras?

Diuitis hoc uitium est auri, nec bella fuerunt
    faginus astabat cum scyphus ante dapes.
non arces, non uallus erat, somnumque petebat
    securus uarias dux gregis inter oues.

Tunc mihi uita foret, Valgi, nec tristia nossem
    arma, nec audissem corde micante tubam.
nunc ad bella trahor, et iam quis forsitan hostis
    haesura in nostro tela gerit latere.

Sed patrii seruate Lares: aluistis et idem
    cursarem uestros cum tener ante pedes.
neu pudeat prisco uos esse e stipite factos:
    sic ueteris sedes incoluistis aui.
tunc melius tenuere fidem cum paupere cultu
    stabat in exigua ligneus aede deus.
hic placatus erat seu quis libauerat uuam
    seu dederat sanctae spicea serta comae;
atque aliquis uoti compos liba ipse ferebat
    postque comes purum filia parua fauum.

At nobis aerata, Lares, depellite tela
    . . . .

. . . .

    hostiaque e plena rustica porcus hara.

80

10

20

Just wait till your replacement takes me prisoner
and proudly rules your kingdom – you'll weep then.
And I'll enjoy your grief and dedicate to Venus
my rescuer a golden leaf of palm inscribed:
TIBULLUS FREED FROM LOVE DECEITFUL, GODDESS,
OFFERS THIS AND ASKS FOR GRATITUDE.

      10

Tell me, who invented the terrifying sword?
Hard he must have been, and truly iron-hearted.
War that day & slaughter were born to humanity;
that day there was opened a short cut to grim death.

Or was the poor wretch blameless? Do we turn against ourselves
the blade intended for wild beasts?

Rich gold – the fault lies there. No wars when stoups of beechwood
stood at the sacrificial feast,
no citadels, no palisades. The leader led a flock
& sued for sleep in safety among the speckled ewes.

O Valgius, were I living then, never had I known
sad arms or heard the trumpet with a pounding heart.
Now I am dragged to war, and some enemy perhaps
already wears the weapon that will pierce my side.

Save me, Lares of my fathers, as you nurtured me
when I ran around in childhood at your feet.
And do not think it shameful to be shaped from an old log:
in that shape you protected my forefathers' estate.
Men kept better faith in the days when wooden gods
humbly decked & tended stood in tiny shrines,
friendly if one gave them the first of the grapes
or bound their sacred locks with spikes of grain;
& the man whose prayer was answered would bring them cakes of meal,
his little daughter following with honey in the comb.

Then turn aside, O Lares, the bronze missiles from us

     .   .   .

& the country offering, a hog from a full sty.

hanc pura cum ueste sequar, myrtoque canistra
    uincta geram, myrto uinctus et ipse caput.
sic placeam uobis. alius sit fortis in armis,
    sternat et aduersos Marte fauente duces,
ut mihi potanti possit sua dicere facta
    miles et in mensa pingere castra mero.

Quis furor est atram bellis accersere Mortem!
    imminet et tacito clam uenit illa pede.
non seges est infra, non uinea culta, sed audax
    Cerberus et Stygiae nauita turpis aquae.
illic percussisque genis ustoque capillo
    errat ad obscuros pallida turba lacus.

Quin potius laudandus hic est quem prole parata
    occupat in parua pigra senecta casa?
ipse suas sectatur oues, at filius agnos;
    et calidam fesso comparat uxor aquam.
sic ego sim, liceatque caput candescere canis,
    temporis et prisci facta referre senem.

Interea Pax arua colat. Pax candida primum
    duxit araturos sub iuga curua boues.
Pax aluit uites et sucos condidit uuae,
    funderet ut nato testa paterna merum.
Pace bidens uomerque nitent, at tristia duri
    militis in tenebris occupat arma situs.
            .   .   .
rusticus e lucoque uehit, male sobrius ipse,
    uxorem plaustro progeniemque domum.
sed Veneris tunc bella calent, scissosque capillos
    femina perfractas conqueriturque fores.
flet teneras subtusa genas, sed uictor et ipse
    flet sibi dementes tam ualuisse manus.
at lasciuus Amor rixae mala uerba ministrat,
    inter et iratum lentus utrumque sedet.

A lapis est ferrumque, suam quicumque puellam
    uerberat: e caelo deripit ille deos.
sit satis e membris tenuem rescindere uestem,
    sit satis ornatus dissoluisse comae,

I shall follow, clad in white, bearing a rush basket
bound with myrtle, wearing a myrtle wreath myself.
So may I find your favour. Others can be brave in arms
& by the grace of Mars cut down the opposing leaders,
to tell me, as I drink, of their exploits in the army
and paint camp on the table-top in wine.

What madness to join forces with sombre Death in war!
Her threat is close, & unperceived her coming.
Below there are no cornfields, no tended vines, but barking
Cerberus & the ugly steersman of the Styx.
There, with cheeks grief-smitten, & with ashen hair,
a pallid multitude drifts by sunless lakes.

But is not the true hero the man slow age surprises
in a little hut with children round him?
He shepherds his own sheep, & his son follows the lambs,
& his wife prepares hot water for the bath.
Such life be mine & with it leave to shine white-haired,
recounting in old age old memories.

Meanwhile let Peace attend the fields. White Peace in the beginning
yoked oxen to the plough
& fed the vines & stored the juices of the grape
for sons to draw wine from their fathers' casks.
In peacetime hoe & ploughshare shine while rust in the dark attacks
the soldier's cruel weapons.

             .   .   .

Home from the sacred grove the farmer far from sober
drives wife and children in the wagon.
Then Venus' war flares up. The woman then bewailing
torn hair & broken door
weeps for soft cheeks bruised, & the winner also weeps
for the mad strength in his hands.
But Love, the mischief-maker, feeds the brawling with abuse
& sits there obstinate between the angry pair.

Ah stone is he & steel who strikes his girl:
he drags down Gods from heaven.
It is enough to rip off the thin dress,
enough to disarrange the well-set hair,

sit lacrimas mouisse satis. quater ille beatus
    cui tenera irato flere puella potest.
sed manibus qui saeuus erit, scutumque sudemque
    is gerat et miti sit procul a Venere.

At nobis, Pax alma, ueni spicamque teneto,
    profluat et pomis candidus ante sinus.

enough to draw her tears. O four times happy he
whose anger makes a tender woman weep!
But the cruel-handed should carry shield & stake
& soldier far away from gentle Venus.

Then come, life-giving Peace, to us, holding the spikes of corn,
& from your white-robed lap let the fruit spill over.

ALBI TIBVLLI ELEGIARVM
LIBER SECVNDVS

ALBIUS TIBULLUS: *ELEGIES*
BOOK TWO

I

Qvisqvis adest, faueat: fruges lustramus et agros,
    ritus ut a prisco traditus exstat auo.
Bacche, ueni dulcisque tuis e cornibus uua
    pendeat, et spicis tempora cinge, Ceres.
luce sacra requiescat humus, requiescat arator,
    et graue suspenso uomere cesset opus.
soluite uincla iugis: nunc ad praesepia debent
    plena coronato stare boues capite.
omnia sint operata deo: non audeat ulla
    lanificam pensis imposuisse manum.
uos quoque abesse procul iubeo, discedat ab aris
    cui tulit hesterna gaudia nocte Venus.
casta placent superis: pura cum ueste uenite
    et manibus puris sumite fontis aquam.

Cernite fulgentes ut eat sacer agnus ad aras
    uinctaque post olea candida turba comas.

Di patrii, purgamus agros, purgamus agrestes:
    uos mala de nostris pellite limitibus.
neu seges eludat messem fallacibus herbis,
    neu timeat celeres tardior agna lupos.
tunc nitidus plenis confisus rusticus agris
    ingeret ardenti grandia ligna foco,
turbaque uernarum, saturi bona signa coloni,
    ludet et ex uirgis exstruet ante casas.

Euentura precor. uiden ut felicibus extis
    significet placidos nuntia fibra deos?

Nunc mihi fumosos ueteris proferte Falernos
    consulis et Chio soluite uincla cado.
uina diem celebrent: non festa luce madere
    est rubor, errantes et male ferre pedes.
sed 'bene Messallam' sua quisque ad pocula dicat,
    nomen et absentis singula uerba sonent.
gentis Aquitanae celeber Messalla triumphis
    et magna intonsis gloria uictor auis,
huc ades aspiraque mihi dum carmine nostro
    redditur agricolis gratia caelitibus.

Keep silence, all: we purify the fruits & fields
according to the usage of our ancestors.
Come, Bacchus, with the sweet grapes hanging from your horns,
& bind your brow with wheaten garland, Ceres.
Let rest the land in holy daylight, let the ploughman rest,
hard labour over, while the share hangs idle.
Unstrap the yokes. Today the oxen are to stand
at laden mangers, garlanded with flowers.
Serve God in every action. Let no woman dare
to lay hand on the daily weight of wool.
I charge all you whom Venus granted joy last night
to stand apart & not approach the altar.
The Gods love purity. Come wearing clean clothes
& take in clean hands water from the spring.

See, the sacred lamb advances to the shining altar,
leading the white procession wreathed with olive.

Gods of our fathers, we purge the fields & the field-workers.
Drive away all evil from our boundaries.
Let no cornland cheat the harvest with deceptive weeds,
no swift wolf terrify the laggard lamb.
Then the cheerful farmer, trusting his full fields,
will pile the fire with large logs, while a troop
of servants' children, token of their master's plenty,
play before it, building houses of sticks.

My prayers are answered: look, the entrails promise well
& the liver's lobe announces Heaven's favour.

Now bring me smoked Falernian, some long-dead consul's vintage.
Unseal a jar of Chian.
Wine to celebrate the day! It is no blushing matter
to drink deep at a feast and walk unsteadily.
But everyone must drink Messalla's health in absence
& every conversation speak his name.
Messalla, famed for triumphs over Aquitanian tribes,
conqueror bringing glory to bearded ancestors,
hither come with inspiration while my song returns
thanks to the Gods of farming.

Rura cano rurisque deos: his uita magistris
    desueuit querna pellere glande famem;
illi compositis primum docuere tigillis
    exiguam uiridi fronde operire domum;
illi etiam tauros primi docuisse feruntur
    seruitium et plaustro supposuisse rotam.
tum uictus abiere feri, tum consita pomus,
    tum bibit irriguas fertilis hortus aquas,
aurea tum pressos pedibus dedit uua liquores
    mixtaque securo est sobria lympha mero.
rura ferunt messes, calidi cum sideris aestu
    deponit flauas annua terra comas;
rure leuis uerno flores apis ingerit alueo,
    compleat ut dulci sedula melle fauos.
agricola assiduo primum satiatus aratro
    cantauit certo rustica uerba pede,
et satur arenti primum est modulatus auena
    carmen, ut ornatos diceret ante deos;
agricola et minio suffusus, Bacche, rubenti
    primus inexperta duxit ab arte choros;
huic datus a pleno memorabile munus ouili
    dux pecoris paruas auxerat hircus opes.
rure puer uerno primum de flore coronam
    fecit et antiquis imposuit Laribus;
rure etiam teneris curam exhibitura puellis
    molle gerit tergo lucida uellus ouis;
hinc et femineus labor est, hinc pensa colusque,
    fusus et apposito pollice uersat opus,
atque aliqua assidue textrix operata Mineruae
    cantat et a pulso tela sonat latere.

Ipse quoque inter agros interque armenta Cupido
    natus et indomitas dicitur inter equas.
illic indocto primum se exercuit arcu:
    ei mihi, quam doctas nunc habet ille manus!
nec pecudes uelut ante petit: fixisse puellas
    gestit et audaces perdomuisse uiros.
hic iuueni detraxit opes, hic dicere iussit
    limen ad iratae uerba pudenda senem;
hoc duce custodes furtim transgressa iacentes
    ad iuuenem tenebris sola puella uenit,

Country I sing & country Gods. Life as their disciple
ceased to drive away hunger with the acorn.
They taught men first to tie rafters together
& roof a little home with green thatch.
They were the first to teach the bull his bondage
& place the wheel beneath the wagon's weight.
Then wild fare was forgotten: fruit-trees then were planted
& kitchen-gardens drank the channeled stream;
then the trampled grapes gave golden liquor;
then sober water mixed with carefree wine.
The country brings us harvest in the shimmering heat
when Earth each year lays down her yellow hair.
In springtime, in the country, light bees are busy bearing
flowers to the hive to fill the combs with honey.
It was a farmer, wearied with continual ploughing,
who first sang country words in fixed metre
& after feasting measured on the first oaten pipe
a tune to play to Gods he had adorned.
A farmer too, O Bacchus, daubed with cinnabar,
improvised your dithyramb, receiving
that memorable trophy from a full fold, the flock's leader,
a he-goat to augment his modest means.
It was a country child first fashioned of spring flowers
a diadem to crown the ancient Lares.
And in the country too, future trouble for tender girls,
soft fleeces line the backs of milk-white sheep.
Hence woman's work, hence woollen stint & distaff,
the spindle twisting yarn beneath the thumb,
the weaver's song, Minerva's constant votary,
& the loom's clatter as the weights collide.

Cupid himself, in fable, was born among the fields,
among the cattle & the wild mares.
There he practised first his unskilled archery.
Alas, how skilful are his hands today!
His aim has shifted from the beasts & now he takes delight
in wounding girls & taming insolent males.
He robs the young of riches & commands the middle-aged
to use unseemly language at an angry's woman's door.
Guided by him the girl steps over sleeping sentries,
creeping to a lover in the lonely dark,

et pedibus praetemptat iter, suspensa timore,
    explorat caecas cui manus ante uias.
a miseri quos hic grauiter deus urget, at ille
    felix cui placidus leniter afflat Amor.   80

Sancte, ueni dapibus festis, sed pone sagittas
    et procul ardentes hinc, precor, abde faces.
uos celebrem cantate deum pecorique uocate:
    uoce palam pecori, clam sibi quisque uocet –
aut etiam sibi quisque palam, nam turba iocosa
    obstrepit et Phrygio tibia curua sono.
ludite: iam Nox iungit equos, currumque sequuntur
    matris lasciuo sidera fulua choro,
postque uenit tacitus, furuis circumdatus alis,
    Somnus, et incerto Somnia nigra pede.   90

        II

Dicamus bona uerba; uenit Natalis ad aras:
    quisquis ades, lingua, uir mulierque, faue.
urantur pia tura focis, urantur odores
    quos tener e terra diuite mittit Arabs.
ipse suos Genius adsit uisurus honores,
    cui decorent sanctas mollia serta comas.
illius puro destillent tempora nardo,
    ille satur libo sit madeatque mero.

Adnuat et, Cornute, tibi quodcumque rogabis.
    en age, quid cessas? adnuit ille – roga.   10
auguror uxoris fidos optabis amores;
    iam reor hoc ipsos edidicisse deos.
nec tibi malueris totum quaecumque per orbem
    fortis arat ualido rusticus arua boue,
nec tibi gemmarum quicquid felicibus Indis
    nascitur, Eoi qua maris unda rubet.

Vota cadunt. uiden ut strepitantibus aduolet alis
    flauaque coniugio uincula portet Amor?
uincula quae maneant semper, dum tarda senectus
    inducat rugas inficiatque comas.   20
eueniat, Natalis, auis prolemque ministret,
    ludat et ante tuos turba nouella pedes.

feeling the way with her feet, pausing on timid tiptoe,
with hand outstretched exploring blind directions.
Wretched they, alas, on whom this God bears hard,
but happy he who feels Love's breath serene.

Come, Holy One, attend our feast, but lay aside your arrows
& far away I pray you hide your blazing torch.
Sing all of you the glorious God & call him to the flock:
call him aloud to the flock, in silence to yourselves –
or even aloud to yourselves, for the din of the merry crowd
& the skirl of the Phrygian pipe will drown the words.
Make sport, for Night already yokes her horses & the yellow
stars in wanton dance attend their mother's car;
& silently behind them, flanked by dusky wings,
comes Sleep – & unsure-footed the black Dreams.

2

Natalis comes to the altar: let us speak no idle word,
but all here present, male & female, guard their tongues.
Burn upon the brazier holy incense, burn the perfumes
which the supple Arab sends from his rich land.
Let the Genius be present to behold the honours paid him
and let soft woollen fillets adorn his hallowed hair.
With oil of spikenard dripping from his temples let him eat
his fill of cake & drink deep of the unmixed wine.

And may he nod assent, Cornutus, to all your requests.
Don't wait, but make them now. Look, he nods assent.
I prophesy that you will pray for a wife's faithful love:
the Gods, I guess, already know that prayer by heart.
Nor would you change your choice for all the cornfields in the world
ploughed by sturdy peasants & the straining ox,
or for all the pearls that grow by India the Blest
where the waves of the Eastern Sea are red as blushes.

Your prayer is granted. Look, a bird on noisy wings flies toward us –
the Love-God, carrying a golden link for marriage!
O may that love-link last for always, till belatedly
old age applies the wrinkles & bedaubs the hair.
Natalis, let the augury come true & bring him offspring
& a troop of little ones play before your feet.

77 *Book Two*

III

Rura meam, Cornute, tenent uillaeque puellam:
  ferreus est, eheu, quisquis in urbe manet.
ipsa Venus latos iam nunc migrauit in agros,
  uerbaque aratoris rustica discit Amor.

O ego dum aspicerem dominam, quam fortiter illic
  uersarem ualido pingue bidente solum,
agricolaeque modo curuum sectarer aratrum,
  dum subigunt steriles arua serenda boues!
nec quererer quod sol graciles exureret artus,
  laederet et teneras pussula rupta manus.   10

Pauit et Admeti tauros formosus Apollo,
  nec cithara intonsae profueruntue comae.
nec potuit curas sanare salubribus herbis:
  quicquid erat medicae uicerat artis amor.
ipse deus solitus stabulis expellere uaccas

    .   .   .

et miscere nouo docuisse coagula lacte,
  lacteus et mixtis obriguisse liquor.
tunc fiscella leui detexta est uimine iunci
  raraque per nexus est uia facta sero.   20
o quotiens illo uitulum gestante per agros
  dicitur occurrens erubuisse soror!
o quotiens ausae, caneret dum ualle sub alta,
  rumpere mugitu carmina docta boues!
saepe duces trepidis petiere oracula rebus,
  uenit et a templis irrita turba domum.
saepe horrere sacros doluit Latona capillos
  quos admirata est ipsa nouerca prius.
quisquis inornatumque caput crinesque solutos
  aspiceret, Phoebi quaereret ille comam.   30
Delos ubi nunc, Phoebe, tua est? ubi Delphica Pytho?
  nempe Amor in parua te iubet esse casa.
felices olim, Veneri cum fertur aperte
  seruire aeternos non puduisse deos!
fabula nunc ille est, sed cui sua cura puella est
  fabula sit mauult quam sine amore deus.

3

Estates & country-houses intern my girl, Cornutus;
only a man of steel could stay in town.
Venus herself has flitted now to lonely fields
& Love is learning ploughman's dialect.

With what determination, if I could see my mistress,
I'd loosen the rich loam with potent mattock
& follow the curved plough in agricultural fashion
while gelded cattle worked the land for sowing,
with never a complaint when the sun scorched my thin arms
or broken blisters made my soft hands sore!

Even fair Apollo fed the cattle of Admetus,
but cithara & long hair did not help,
nor could he cure his cares with therapeutic herbs,
for Love defeated all his skill in medicine.
Himself, albeit God, he drove cows from a byre

        .   .   .

& to have taught the mixing of rennet with fresh milk,
coagulating thus the milky mixture.
Frails were woven then of the light stems of rushes
& space left in the tight weave for the whey.
O how many times his sister blushed to meet him
carrying a bull-calf home through the fields,
or while he sang in some deep valley, cows presumed
to interrupt his music with their moos!
Leaders in time of crisis sought his oracles
& trooped home disappointed from the shrine.
The sacred locks that even Juno used to envy
in disarray dismayed his mother Leto.
Anyone who saw the shaggy head & tousled tresses
must have looked in vain for Apollo's hair-style.
O Phoebus, where is Delos now, & where your Delphic Pytho?
Love commands your presence in a little hut.
Happy those prehistoric days when the immortal Gods
were not ashamed to be the public slaves of Venus!
Apollo is a byword now, but any lovelorn mortal
would sooner be a byword than a God unloved.

At tu, quisquis is es, cui tristi fronte Cupido
    imperat ut nostra sint tua castra domo

          .   .   .

ferrea non Venerem sed praedam saecula laudant;
    praeda tamen multis est operata malis.   40
praeda feras acies cinxit discordibus armis:
    hinc cruor, hinc caedes mors propiorque uenit.
praeda uago iussit geminare pericula ponto,
    bellica cum dubiis rostra dedit ratibus.
praedator cupit inmensos obsidere campos
    ut multa innumera iugera pascat oue;
cui lapis externus curae est urbisque tumultu
    portatur ualidis mille columna iugis,
claudit et indomitum moles mare, lentus ut intra
    neglegat hibernas piscis adesse minas.   50

At mihi laeta trahant Samiae conuiuia testae
    fictaque Cumana lubrica terra rota.
eheu diuitibus uideo gaudere puellas:
    iam ueniant praedae si Venus optat opes,
ut mea luxuria Nemesis fluat utque per urbem
    incedat donis conspicienda meis.
illa gerat uestes tenues quas femina Coa
    texuit, auratas disposuitque uias.
illi sint comites fusci quos India torret,
    Solis et admotis inficit ignis equis.   60
illi selectos certent praebere colores
    Africa puniceum purpureumque Tyros.

Vota loquor: regnum ille tenet quem saepe coegit
    barbara gypsatos ferre catasta pedes.

At tibi, dura Ceres, Nemesim quae abducis ab urbe,
    persoluat nulla semina terra fide.
et tu, Bacche tener, iucundae consitor uuae,
    tu quoque deuotos, Bacche, relinque lacus.
haud impune licet formosas tristibus agris
    abdere: non tanti sunt tua musta, Pater.   70
o ualeant fruges, ne sint modo rure puellae.
    glans alat et prisco more bibantur aquae.
glans aluit ueteres, et passim semper amarunt.
    quid nocuit sulcos non habuisse satos?

But you, the anonymous, whom Cupid's frowning brow
commands to make my home your camp

      .   .   .

Not Love but Loot our iron age applauds:
but Loot works many evils.
Loot equips fierce battle-lines with jarring arms;
hence bloodshed, slaughter, sudden death.
Loot has doubled danger on the fickle deep
by giving unsafe galleys beaks of war.
The Looter longs to own measureless plains & pasture
wide acres with innumerable sheep.
He fancies foreign marble & yokes a thousand oxen
to cart his columns, setting Rome in turmoil.
He pens the open sea with moles to make a pond
where cold-eyed fish can disregard the storm.

Though I'm content with Samian ware to extend a merry party
or cups of clay turned on the wheels of Cumae,
alas, there's no denying that girls adore the rich.
Then welcome Loot if Love loves affluence.
My Nemesis shall float in luxury & strut
the Roman streets parading gifts of mine.
She shall wear fine silks woven by women of Cos
& bordered with threads of gold.
She shall have swart attendants, browned in India,
stained by the Sun-God steering near.
Let Africa with scarlet & with purple Tyre
compete to offer her their choicest dyes.

My words are day-dreams. Now her king's a former slave, who once
marked time with chalked feet on a foreign scaffold.

Ah Ceres, cruel temptress of my Nemesis from Rome,
may earth break faith & pay you back short seed.
And you, O tender Bacchus, planter of the pleasant vine,
curse those wine-vats & abandon them.
It's a punishable trespass to hide Beauty in dull fields:
your vintage, Father Bacchus, costs too much.
Fruits of the earth, farewell, if you keep girls on the land.
Let us live on acorns & drink old-fashioned water.
The men of old made love on acorns any time or place,
lost nothing by not having furrows for the seed.

tum, quibus aspirabat Amor, praebebat aperte
    mitis in umbrosa gaudia ualle Venus.
nullus erat custos, nulla exclusura dolentes
    ianua. si fas est, mos, precor, ille redi.

    . . .

horrida uillosa corpora ueste tegant.   80
nunc, si clausa mea est, si copia rara uidendi,
    heu miserum laxam quid iuuat esse togam?
ducite. ad imperium dominae sulcabimus agros:
    non ego me uinclis uerberibusque nego.

  IV

Sic mihi seruitium uideo dominamque paratam:
    iam mihi, libertas illa paterna, uale.
seruitium sed triste datur, teneorque catenis,
    et numquam misero uincla remittit Amor,
et seu quid merui seu nil peccauimus, urit.
    uror: io, remoue, saeua puella, faces.

O ego ne possim tales sentire dolores,
    quam mallem in gelidis montibus esse lapis!
stare uel insanis cautes obnoxia uentis,
    naufraga quam uasti tunderet unda maris!   10
nunc et amara dies et noctis amarior umbra est;
    omnia nunc tristi tempora felle madent.
nec prosunt elegi nec carminis auctor Apollo:
    illa caua pretium flagitat usque manu.

Ite procul, Musae, si non prodestis amanti:
    non ego uos ut sint bella canenda colo,
nec refero Solisque uias et qualis, ubi orbem
    compleuit, uersis Luna recurrit equis.
ad dominam faciles aditus per carmina quaero:
    ite procul, Musae, si nihil ista ualent.   20

At mihi per caedem et facinus sunt dona paranda,
    ne iaceam clausam flebilis ante domum.
aut rapiam suspensa sacris insignia fanis:
    sed Venus ante alios est uiolanda mihi.
illa malum facinus suadet dominamque rapacem
    dat mihi: sacrilegas sentiat illa manus.

In their day gentle Venus in every shady valley
provided Love's enthusiasts with public joy.
No guard was there or door to bar the broken-hearted.
May God reintroduce that ancient custom.

     .   .   .

Let them cover hairy nakedness with pelts.
But if my girl's a prisoner now & I can rarely see her,
what good to me, alas, is a toga flowing free?
Lead on. I'll plough the furrows at the bidding of a mistress
& cheerfully accept the leg-irons & the lash.

     4

Slave to a mistress! Yes, in recognition of my fate
bidding now farewell to the freedom of my birthright
I accept the harshest slavery – for I am held in chains
& never, to my sorrow, does Love relax the bonds.
He burns me too, regardless of my guilt or innocence.
I'm burning now. Ai-ee, cruel girl, remove the torch!

O that I need never experience this torment
I'd sooner be a stone on some cold mountainside
or standing rock exposed to mad gales, buffeted
by the lonely sea's ship-splintering waves!
Bitter now the daylight, still more bitter the dark night;
every moment now is soaked in sour gall.
Elegies & Phoebus, poets' patron, are no help:
my lady cups her hand & keeps demanding cash.

Leave me alone, O Muses, if you cannot help a lover.
I do not ask your aid to sing of epic wars
nor do I track the Sun-God's path or tell of how the Moon,
her round completed, turns her steeds & gallops back.
By poetry I look for easy access to a mistress.
Leave me alone, O Muses, if your magic does not work.

I must take to crime & bloodshed to provide her with the gifts
that save me from those weeping vigils at her door;
or steal the sacred offerings hung up on temple walls:
& Venus shall be first to be profaned.
She tempts me to do evil & devotes me to a grasping
mistress; she deserves to suffer sacrilege.

O pereat quicumque legit uiridesque smaragdos
    et niueam Tyrio murice tingit ouem!
hic dat auaritiae causas et Coa puellis
    uestis et e Rubro lucida concha Mari.   30
haec fecere malas, hinc clauim ianua sensit
    et coepit custos liminis esse canis.
sed pretium si grande feras, custodia uicta est
    nec prohibent claues et canis ipse tacet.
heu quicumque dedit formam caelestis auarae,
    quale bonum multis attulit ille malis!
hinc fletus rixaeque sonant, haec denique causa
    fecit ut infamis nunc deus esset Amor.

At tibi quae pretio uictos excludis amantes
    eripiant partas uentus et ignis opes.   40
quin, tua tunc iuuenes spectent incendia laeti
    nec quisquam flammae sedulus addat aquam.
heu, ueniet tibi mors, nec erit qui lugeat ullus
    nec qui det maestas munus in exsequias.

At bona quae nec auara fuit, centum licet annos
    uixerit, ardentem flebitur ante rogum;
atque aliquis senior, ueteres ueneratus amores,
    annua constructo serta dabit tumulo,
et 'bene' discedens dicet 'placideque quiescas,
    terraque securae sit super ossa leuis.'   50

Vera quidem moneo, sed prosunt quid mihi uera?
    illius est nobis lege colendus Amor.
quin etiam sedes iubeat si uendere auitas,
    ite sub imperium sub titulumque, Lares.
quicquid habet Circe, quicquid Medea ueneni,
    quicquid et herbarum Thessala terra gerit,
et quod, ubi indomitis gregibus Venus afflat amores,
    hippomanes cupidae stillat ab inguine equae,
si modo me placido uideat Nemesis mea uultu,
    mille alias herbas misceat illa, bibam.   60

                    V

Phoebe, faue: nouus ingreditur tua templa sacerdos:
    huc, age, cum cithara carminibusque ueni.

Death to all the dealers in green emerald, to all
who stain the snow-white wool with purple dyes of Tyre.
They & Coan silks & lucent pearls from the Red Sea –
these are the incentives of avarice in girls.
This is why they're faithless, why the key twists in the lock,
& why the keeper of the door's a dog.
But if you bring big money, the keeper keeps away,
the key turns over, even the dog is dumb.
Alas, whichever God it was gave grasping woman beauty,
what a good he added to a mort of ill!
Hence the noisy tears & quarrels; here the reason why
Love is now a God of evil reputation.

But you who lock out lovers outbidden in your auction,
may wind & fire rob you of the money you've amassed
& may the young men laugh to see your goods ablaze
& no one help throw water on the flames.
Death, alas, will come for you, but there'll be none to mourn
or share the cost of your sad funeral.

But any kind & generous girl can live a hundred years
& tears will still be shed beside her pyre.
Some elder man in fond remembrance of his former love
each year will bring her flowers to the grave
& as he leaves will say 'Sleep soundly & in peace,
& earth be light on your untroubled bones.'

True prophecy. And yet what help to the true prophet?
Love's worship means obedience to her laws.
Why, even if she bade me sell my ancestral home
I'd pack the Lares off under a bill of sale.
All Circe's magic potions, all Medea's drugs
& all the herbs that sprout in Thessaly,
horse-madness too, that exudation from the mare in season
when Venus breathes her longing into the wild herds,
& a thousand other simples, brewed by Nemesis, I'd drink
if only to find favour in her eyes.

    5

Bless, O Phoebus, the new priest entering your temple;
make haste & hither come with psalm & cithara.

nunc te uocales impellere pollice chordas,
  nunc precor ad laudes flectere uerba mea.
ipse triumphali deuinctus tempora lauro
  dum cumulant aras ad tua sacra ueni.
sed nitidus pulcherque ueni: nunc indue uestem
  sepositam, longas nunc bene pecte comas,
qualem te memorant Saturno rege fugato
  uictori laudes concinuisse Ioui.   10

Tu procul euentura uides, tibi deditus augur
  scit bene quid fati prouida cantet auis;
tuque regis sortes, per te praesentit haruspex
  lubrica signauit cum deus exta notis;
te duce Romanis numquam frustrata Sibylla,
  abdita quae senis fata canit pedibus.
Phoebe, sacras Messallinum sine tangere chartas
  uatis, et ipse, precor, quid canat illa doce.

Haec dedit Aeneae sortes postquam ille parentem
  dicitur et raptos sustinuisse Lares.   20
nec fore credebat Romam cum maestus ab alto
  Ilion ardentes respiceretque deos.
Romulus aeternae nondum formauerat Vrbis
  moenia, consorti non habitanda Remo,
sed tunc pascebant herbosa Palatia uaccae
  et stabant humiles in Iouis arce casae.
lacte madens illic suberat Pan ilicis umbrae
  et facta agresti lignea falce Pales,
pendebatque uagi pastoris in arbore uotum
  garrula siluestri fistula sacra deo,   30
fistula cui semper decrescit harundinis ordo,
  nam calamus cera iungitur usque minor.
at qua Velabri regio patet, ire solebat
  exiguus pulsa per uada linter aqua.
illac saepe gregis diti placitura magistro
  ad uillam festa est uecta puella die,
cum qua fecundi redierunt munera ruris,
  caseus et niueae candidus agnus ouis.

'Impiger Aenea, uolitantis frater Amoris,
  Troica qui profugis sacra uehis ratibus,   40

Pluck now, I pray you, with your thumb the singing strings
& tune my utterance to hymns of praise.
Bind your brow with bays triumphant: come among us,
while they heap the altar, for your sacrifice.
In brightness & in beauty come, putting on today
the robe of state & combing your luxuriant hair,
as on that legendary day when Saturn fled his kingdom
& you sang the glory of victorious Jove.

You see the future from afar. Your votary the augur
understands the song of the prophetic bird.
You rule the lots. Through you the soothsayer interprets
the signature of God on slippery entrails.
Inspired by you the Sibyl singing destiny obscure
in Greek hexameters has never failed the Romans.
O Phoebus, grant that Messallinus touch her sacred scrolls
& teach him, I beseech you, the meaning of her song.

She gave Aeneas oracles, after (as legend tells)
he carried father & homeless Gods to safety,
incredulous of future Rome when from the deep in grief
he gazed at Troy & Trojan temples burning.
Not yet had Romulus drawn up the Eternal City's walls,
where Remus as co-ruler was fated not to live;
but cows were grazing then a grassy Palatine
& hovels raised low roofs on the hill of Jove.
There drenched with milk was Pan, half seen in ilex shade,
& wooden Pales hewn by rustic hook,
& on the tree in dedication to Silvanus
hung a wandering shepherd's tuneful pipe,
the pipe with reeds set in descending order,
each stalk wax-welded to a shorter one.
But where today Velabrum stretches, little dinghies
plied across a shallow lake: that way
the future mistress of the flock's rich master
voyaged on a feast day to his farm,
returning with the gifts of country plenty,
cheeses & a snowy ewe's white lamb.

'Unwearying Aeneas, brother of winged Love,
sailing with Ilium's sacred gear in exile,

iam tibi Laurentes assignat Iuppiter agros,
    iam uocat errantes hospita terra Lares.
illic sanctus eris cum te ueneranda Numici
    unda deum caelo miserit indigetem.

Ecce, super fessas uolitat Victoria puppes:
    tandem ad Troianos diua superba uenit.
ecce, mihi lucent Rutulis incendia castris:
    iam tibi praedico, barbare Turne, necem.
ante oculos Laurens castrum murusque Lauini est
    Albaque ab Ascanio condita Longa duce.   50
te quoque iam uideo, Marti placitura sacerdos,
    Ilia, Vestales deseruisse focos,
concubitusque tuos furtim, uittasque iacentes,
    et cupidi ad ripas arma relicta dei.

Carpite nunc, tauri, de septem montibus herbas
    dum licet: hic magnae iam locus urbis erit.
Roma, tuum nomen terris fatale regendis
    qua sua de caelo prospicit arua Ceres,
quaque patent ortus et qua fluitantibus undis
    Solis anhelantes abluit amnis equos.   60
Troia quidem tunc se mirabitur et sibi dicet
    uos bene tam longa consuluisse uia.
uera cano: sic usque sacras innoxia laurus
    uescar et aeternum sit mihi uirginitas.'
haec cecinit uates et te sibi, Phoebe, uocauit,
    iactauit fusas et caput ante comas.

Quicquid Amalthea, quicquid Marpesia dixit
    Herophile, Phoeto Graia quod admonuit,
quasque Aniena sacras Tiburs per flumina sortes
    portarat sicco pertuleratque sinu –   70
haec fore dixerunt belli mala signa cometen,
    multus ut in terras deplueretque lapis.
atque tubas atque arma ferunt strepitantia caelo
    audita, et lucos praecinuisse fugam.
ipsum etiam Solem, defectum lumine, uidit
    iungere pallentes nubilus annus equos,
et simulacra deum lacrimas fudisse tepentes,
    fataque uocales praemonuisse boues.

now Jupiter apportions you Laurentine fields
& welcome land invites your wandering Lares.
There you shall be hallowed when Numicus' holy stream
to heaven sends you as a hero-god.

See where Victory hovers over your worn fleet – at last
the overbearing goddess stoops to Trojans.
See where fire blazes in the encampment of the Rutuli,
foreboding sudden death for savage Turnus.
Laurentum's fort, Lavinium's wall are there before my eyes,
& Alba Longa, founded by Ascanius.
Ilia also I behold, the priestess loved by Mars,
her dereliction of the Vestal hearth,
her secret intercourse, the sacred fillet thrown aside
with the lustful God's armour on the bank.

Crop while ye may, O bulls, the grass on the Seven Hills:
here shall be the site of a mighty city –
Rome, the name predestined for empire of the world
where Ceres looks from heaven upon her fields,
where rising up the Sun-God spreads his beams & where in Ocean's
tidal stream he bathes his panting steeds.
Then truly Troy in self-amaze will tell herself
you served her well by so long wandering.
It is the truth I sing – so may I feed unscathed
on sacred bay & be forever virgin.'
Thus sang the Sibyl, Phoebus, & called you to her aid
tossing the long loose hair over her eyes.

The rede of Amalthea & Marpessian Herophile,
the admonitions of Hellenic Phoeto,
the sacred lots which Tibur's Sibyl carried as she swam
down the Anio & brought them dry to land –
all these foretold a comet, the wicked sign of war,
& a rain of stones falling on the earth.
Men say the clang of arms was heard & trumpets in the sky
& voices from the sacred groves forechanting rout.
That year of cloud beheld even the Sun himself
harnessing pale horses in eclipse,
& images of Gods that shed warm tears,
& cattle speaking, prophesying doom.

haec fuerunt olim, sed tu iam mitis, Apollo,
  prodigia indomitis merge sub aequoribus.   80

Vt succensa sacris crepitat bene laurea flammis!
  omine quo felix et satur annus erit.
laurus ubi bona signa dedit, gaudete, coloni:
  distendet spicis horrea plena Ceres,
oblitus et musto feriet pede rusticus uuas
  dolia dum magni deficiantque lacus,
ac madidus Baccho sua festa, Palilia, pastor
  concinet (a stabulis tunc procul este, lupi).
ille leuis stipulae sollemnes potus aceruos
  accendet, flammas transilietque sacras,   90
et fetus matrona dabit, natusque parenti
  oscula comprensis auribus eripiet,
nec taedebit auum paruo aduigilare nepoti
  balbaque cum puero dicere uerba senem.
tunc operata deo pubes discumbet in herba,
  arboris antiquae qua leuis umbra cadit,
aut e ueste sua tendent umbracula sertis
  uincta, coronatus stabit et ipse calix.
at sibi quisque dapes et festas exstruet alte
  caespitibus mensas caespitibusque torum.   100
ingeret hic potus iuuenis maledicta puellae
  postmodo quae uotis irrita facta uelit;
nam ferus ille suae plorabit sobrius idem
  et se iurabit mente fuisse mala.

Pace tua pereant arcus pereantque sagittae,
  Phoebe, modo in terris erret inermis Amor.
ars bona, sed postquam sumpsit sibi tela Cupido,
  eheu quam multis ars dedit ista malum!
et mihi praecipue, iaceo cum saucius annum
  et faueo morbo – quin iuuat ipse dolor.   110
usque cano Nemesim, sine qua uersus mihi nullus
  uerba potest iustos aut reperire pedes.

At tu, nam diuum seruat tutela poetas,
  praemoneo, uati parce puella sacro,
ut Messallinum celebrem cum praemia belli
  ante suos currus oppida uicta feret,

These omens came to pass of old, but now in mercy, Phoebus,
drown prodigies beneath the untamed sea.

How the kindled bayleaves crackle in the sacred flames,
promising a year fortunate & fruitful!
Rejoice, you tenant-farmers, when the bay gives lucky signs,
for Ceres will cram full your granaries with grain,
& peasants daubed with wine-lees will trample out the grapes
till vat & ample cistern overflow.
Shepherds also drinking deep will sing at the Palilia
their special feast (that day let wolves avoid the fold!)
& when they're drunk will set alight the customary heaps
of straw & overleap them through the sacred flames.
Then Roman wives will all be mothers & the growing boy
will grip his father's ears & steal a kiss.
Grandfathers will be glad to take full charge of little grandsons
& old men talk with children in child language.
Then serving God the folk will lie in groups upon the grass
where lightly falls the shadow of an ancient tree,
or spread their cloaks as canopies & garland them with flowers
& decorate the wine-bowls too with chaplets.
Everyone will pile his plate with food & build up high
a table & a dining-couch of turf;
& here the youth will fling drunken curses at his girl
which later he will wish made void by lover's vows,
weeping when he's sober at his former beastliness
& swearing he was out of his right mind.

O Phoebus, by your leave, perish bow & perish arrows
if only Love can wend his devious way unarmed.
Art is good, but after Cupid took to archery,
alas, how much misfortune your archer's art has brought!
On me especially, for I have lain a year now stricken,
clinging to my sickness, finding pleasure in the pain,
singing of my Nemesis, without whom not one line
of mine can rediscover true rhythm or right phrase.

But since divine protection watches over poets,
pray take pity, sweetheart, on a sacred bard,
so that I may sing of Messallinus when he drives
the spoils of conquered towns before his chariot,

ipse gerens laurus, lauro deuinctus agresti
    miles 'io' magna uoce 'Triumphe' canet.
tunc Messalla meus pia det spectacula turbae
    et plaudat curru praetereunte pater.
annue: sic tibi sint intonsi, Phoebe, capilli,
    sit tua perpetuo sic tibi casta soror.

VI

Castra Macer sequitur: tenero quid fiet Amori?
    sit comes et collo fortiter arma gerat?
et seu longa uirum terrae uia seu uaga ducent
    aequora, cum telis ad latus ire uolet?
ure, puer, quaeso, tua qui ferus otia liquit,
    atque iterum erronem sub tua signa uoca.
quod si militibus parces, erit hic quoque miles,
    ipse leuem galea qui sibi portet aquam.
castra peto, ualeatque Venus ualeantque puellae:
    et mihi sunt uires, et mihi facta tuba est.

Magna loquor, sed magnifice mihi magna locuto
    excutiunt clausae fortia uerba fores.
iuraui quotiens rediturum ad limina numquam!
    cum bene iuraui, pes tamen ipse redit.
acer Amor, fractas utinam tua tela sagittas,
    si licet, extinctas aspiciamque faces!
tu miserum torques, tu me mihi dira precari
    cogis et insana mente nefanda loqui.

Iam mala finissem leto, sed credula uitam
    Spes fouet et fore cras semper ait melius.
Spes alit agricolas, Spes sulcis credit aratis
    semina quae magno faenore reddat ager.
haec laqueo uolucres, haec captat harundine pisces
    cum tenues hamos abdidit ante cibus.
Spes etiam ualida solatur compede uinctum:
    crura sonant ferro, sed canit inter opus.
Spes facilem Nemesim spondet mihi, sed negat illa:
    ei mihi, ne uincas, dura puella, deam.

Parce, per immatura tuae precor ossa sororis:
    sic bene sub tenera parua quiescat humo.

crowned with bay himself, his troops with wild bay garlanded,
chanting in loud voices the ritual Triumph cry.
Then let my Messalla give the crowd a fond display
by cheering as his son's chariot passes by.
O Phoebus, grant me this, & may your locks remain unshorn
& your sister virgin to the end of time.

6

Macer joins the army. What will tender Love do now?
Go with him as comrade, shouldering a pack,
bearing arms beside a mortal on the endless road
leading over land & never-resting sea?
No, Cupid: brand the ruffian who has left your life of leisure,
recalling the deserter to the flag of love.
But if you're lenient to soldiers, I will soldier too,
carrying the ration of water in my casque.
I'm off to camp & bid goodbye to Venus & the girls.
I too can take the trumpet; I too can be tough.

Brave words, but when I've said them with magnificent bravado
the slamming of a door sends every brave word flying.
I've sworn so often nevermore to set foot on her doorstep,
but after all the swearing my feet still take me there.
O cruel Love, if it be lawful, let me see your weapons,
the arrows & the torches, broken & burnt out.
You torture my unhappiness. You make me curse myself
& with a mind unbalanced utter blasphemy.

Death would have ended my distress but Hope's credulity
nurses life & says 'Tomorrow will be better.'
Hope feeds the farmer. Hope entrusts the furrow with a loan
of seed to be repaid at compound interest.
Hope entices birds with snares & fish with rods of reed
hiding a thin hook underneath the bait.
Hope comforts even those whose legs are bound in heavy fetters;
the iron clanks on their ankles but while they work they sing.
Hope guarantees me Nemesis, but Nemesis says No.
Ah, cruel girl, you ought to let a goddess win.

Take pity, I implore you, by your little sister's bones:
so may the child sleep softly under gentle earth.

illa mihi sancta est, illius dona sepulcro
    et madefacta meis serta feram lacrimis,
illius ad tumulum fugiam supplexque sedebo
    et mea cum muto fata querar cinere.
non feret usque suum te propter flere clientem:
    illius ut uerbis, sis mihi lenta ueto,
ne tibi neglecti mittant mala somnia Manes
    maestaque sopitae stet soror ante torum,
qualis ab excelsa praeceps delapsa fenestra
    uenit ad infernos sanguinolenta lacus.   40

Desino, ne dominae luctus renouentur acerbi:
    non ego sum tanti, ploret ut illa semel,
nec lacrimis oculos digna est foedare loquaces.
    lena nocet nobis; ipsa puella bona est.
lena uetat miserum Phryne, furtimque tabellas
    occulto portans itque reditque sinu.
saepe ego cum dominae dulces a limine duro
    agnosco uoces, haec negat esse domi.
saepe ubi nox mihi promissa est, languere puellam
    nuntiat aut aliquas extimuisse minas.   50
tunc morior curis, tunc mens mihi perdita fingit
    quisue meam teneat quot teneatue modis;
tunc tibi, lena, precor diras: satis anxia uiuas,
    mouerit e uotis pars quotacumque deos.

I hold her sacred & will lay upon her burial-mound
offerings & a garland sprinkled with my tears.
I'll fly for refuge to the grave, sit there a suppliant
& to her dumb ashes utter my complaint.
She will not suffer me to weep on your account for ever.
In her name I forbid you to use me heartlessly,
for fear the blessed dead rejected send you evil dreams
& you behold her standing by your bed in grief,
just as when she fell head foremost from the upper window
& went with blood upon her to the lakes below.

Enough, lest I renew the bitter sorrow of my mistress;
that she should weep once only is more than I am worth.
Nor ought she to disfigure her clear-speaking eyes with tears:
the bawd is my undoing; my girl herself is good.
Phryne the bawd debars me as she slily comes & goes
bearing in her bosom secret messages.
On the cruel threshold often I can recognise
the sweet voice of my mistress when Phryne says she's out.
Often, when a night is promised, Phryne brings me word
my girl's unwell or victim of intimidation.
I die then of frustration & despairingly imagine
who's embracing her & in how many ways.
Bawd, I curse you then, & pain enough would be your life
were the Gods to grant the least of all my prayers.

EPITAPHIVM TIBVLLI

Te quoque Vergilio comitem non aequa, Tibulle,
   Mors iuuenem campos misit ad Elysios,
ne foret aut elegis molles qui fleret amores
   aut caneret forti regia bella pede.

VITA TIBVLLI

Albius Tibullus, eques Romanus, insignis forma cultuque corporis obseruabilis, ante alios Coruinum Messallam oratorem dilexit, cuius etiam contubernalis Aquitanico bello militaribus donis donatus est. hic multorum iudicio principem inter elegiographos optinet locum. epistolae quoque eius amatoriae, quamquam breues, omnino utiles sunt. obiit adulescens, ut indicat epigramma suprascriptum.

TIBULLUS'S EPITAPH

Inequitable Death sent you, Tibullus, also
as Virgil's comrade young to Elysian Fields,
lest any live to weep soft loves in elegiacs
or sing of royal wars in brave rhythm.

THE LIFE

Albius Tibullus, Roman knight, noted for good looks and remark-
able for personal adornment, beyond others loved Corvinus Messalla
the orator, as whose aide also in the Aquitanian War he was awarded
military decorations. In the judgement of many he occupies first place
among the elegiographers. His amatory epistles too, though short,
are thoroughly useful. He died young, as the epigram quoted above
testifies.

NOTES

TEXTUAL NOTES

The editor of a literary text is also a scribe who must copy, or otherwise reproduce, his text for the printer from some reliable source, printed or in manuscript. I accordingly chose to type out the text of Tibullus from a photograph of the earliest MS, the Ambrosian of 1374 (*R 26 sup.* in the Biblioteca Ambrosiana, Milan, discovered by Baehrens in 1876), simply recording departures from it – some 240 in all – in the list that follows. To settle questions about first & second hands I examined the actual MS.

For the readings of other MSS, readings which, though appearing in my text, for the sake of brevity are not attributed to their source, I have used photographs of the Vaticanus, the next earliest MS (3270 in the Vatican Library), of the Guelferbytanus, an important 15th century MS (*Aug. 82.6. fol.* in the Herzog August Library at Wolfenbüttel), & of the 10th century Freising Excerpts (6292 in the Bavarian State Library, Munich). For the rest, including the conjectures of scholars, I have relied on the critical apparatuses of Calonghi (1928) and Lenz–Galinsky (1971).

The punctuation is modern. The spelling has been brought into line with what may be called the vulgate orthography. Spelling departures from the Ambrosian are not listed (this includes *tum* for *tunc* & *eheu* for *heu heu*), nor do I record the unimportant spelling mistakes of my source (e.g. 1.2.54 *perdonuisse*, 1.5.65 *ocultos*).

With these omissions the readings quoted below are those of the Ambrosian. When the reading printed in my text is not found in a MS, the name of the scholar whom I believe to have first conjectured it is given; a colon separates this name from the Ambrosian reading. Where there might be doubt which word in the Latin text replaces the Ambrosian reading, that word is quoted & followed either by a square bracket or by a scholar's name. My own emendations are attributed to *Translator*.

1   14 agricolae   19 felices   24 clamat   25 non possum   29 ludentes   37 et
44 scilicet   49 si   54 exiles   59 & 60 te] et   63 dura   64 iuncta
73 posses

2   23 decet   42 rapido   60 ipse   67 possit   71 contextus   80 posset
81 magni   84 diripuisse   89 *Broukhusius*: laetus   90 unus

3   9 quam *Dousa pater*: cum   12 *Muretus*: triuiis   13 numquam
14 *Aldine edition 1502*: cum   17 aues dant
18 *Some 16th century scholar*: Saturni   21 neu   22 *Doering*: sciat   25 deum
38 ueteris   50 reperte   81–2 *Camps*: uiolauit . . . optauit   86 colo
91 nunc

4   8 sit   28 remeatque   29 te perdit   36 illam   40 credas   44 *Crux as yet
unsolved*   53 mihi . . . cum   54 *Santen*: tamen apta   59 at] iam   62 ne
63 est *omitted*   71 *Heyne*: Venus ipsa   72 flentibus   80 diducat
81 heheu

5   1 dissidium   2 sortis   3 turbo   6 post haec   7 per te] parce
16 uoca nouem creme   28 segete et spicas   30 adiuuet
35 *Roman edition 1475*: Eurus   42 *Lucian Mueller*: et pudet. *Nodell*: mea
45 Nereis quae   47 nunc *Translator*: huic   55 *Castiglioni*: urbes
60 *Huschke*: nam   61 *Muretus*: praesto tibi praesto   67 iuncta   69 furta
74 usque] ipse   76 nat] nam

6   11 nunc   18 lasso   21 *Achilles Statius*: quam   40 effluit
42 *Another crux. I supply* transeat ille *to make a readable text*: stet procul
ante   45 mota   46 non et amans   47 uiolata   52 *Achilles Statius*:
didicisse   55 *Baehrens*: -quas . . . poenas   67 uicta   70 possum
71 putat ducor   72 proprias proripiorque   84 quam] quod

7   4 *Scaliger*: Atax   6 uinctos   9 *Scaliger*: tua bella   12 Carnoti   13 at
14 *Voss*: placidis . . . aquis   16 arat   27 *Platnauer*: atque   40 *Muretus*:
tristitiae   42 cuspide   49 *Markland*: centum ludos   54 Mosopio . . . mella
57 ne . . . quae   61 canit. *Baehrens added* a

8   1 celare   2 ferat . . . leuia   11 comas   29 ne   36 *Heyne*: conserit
49 seu   51 sentita   52 luteo   53 heu *Camps*: uel   57 leuis
59 *Kraffert*: quamuis   61 possunt   64 *Francken*: est . . . euigilanda
77 *P. Burman II*: at

9   9 petituros   19 O uiciis   23 celanti fas   24 sit . . . uetet
25 saepe *Muretus*: leue   31 nullo tibi   35 eriperet   36 *Heyne*: puras
40 sit . . . sed   44 sed . . . clausos   48 *Translator*: et me   68 pectore
69 *Postgate*: ista   73 nec] haec   75 huic] hunc. *And* illum *Translator for*
hunc   81 dum

10 8 ciphus   11 *Heyne*: uulgi   18 ueteres   21 uua   23 ipsa   30 aduerso
36 puppis   49 uidens (*corrected to* nitens) uomer uiderit. *Guyet proposed*
nitent   51 elutoque . . . ipso   60 diripit   61 perscindere   64 quo
68 praefluat

BOOK TWO

1 1 *Scaliger*: ualeat   9 sunt   23 satiri   34 *Scaliger*: ades   38 grande famen
42 suppotuisse   45 antea tunc   49 ingerat   50 et   54 duceret
58 *Postgate & others*: yrcus hauxerat hyrcus oues   65 Mineruam
66 *Muretus*: appulso   73 opus   74 limem   88 thoro   89 fuluis

2 7 distillent   8 *Translator*: atque   15 undis   17 utinam   19 uinculaque
21 *Housman*: hic ueniat

3 5 dum *Heyne*: cum   11 armenti   18 *Muretus*: mixtus   37 est   45 obsistere
46 et   47 tumulti   51 tibi   57 gerit   63 uota *Kraus*: nota liquor. *And*
ille . . . quem *Guyet*: ipse . . . quae   64 bipsatos   65 *Heinsius*: seges
Nemesis qui abducit   72 et *omitted*   82 iuuet

4 2 pater ue   4 remittet   5 nil *Heinsius*: quid   10 uasti *omitted*   12 nam
17 equalis . . . urbem   33 uicta] incerta   36 ipse   38 nunc *Broukhusius*: hic
40 portas   43 *Camps*: seu   44 obsequias   55 quidquam habet
59 modo] non

5 4 *Lachmann*: meas   11 debitus   18 quos canat   20 captos   34 pulla
35 *Rossbach*: illaque. *Muretus*: ditis   36 *Camps*: ad iuuenem   47 rutilis
49 castris   62 longam . . . uiam   64 noscar   68 *Lachmann*: Phoebo grata
69 quodque Albana sacras Tiberis   70 *Postgate*: portarit . . . perluerit
72 et . . . deplueritque   76 amnis   79 fuerant   81 crepitet
82 *Cornelissen*: sacer   92 compressis   94 puro   95 operta   99 extruat
109 taceo   110 *Leo*: cum   116 ferent   122 perpetua. *And* sit . . . sic tibi
Translator for sic . . . sit tibi

6 16 scilicet   32 ferant   45 Phirne   46 itque] tuncque   47 diro

Romanus] regalis. *Baehrens' conjecture* Romanus e Gabis *may be right.*
oratorem] originem   equitanico   superscriptum

EXPLANATORY NOTES

1.4   Cf. Bacchylides *Fragment* 4.35–7 (in praise of Peace) 'There is no din of brazen trumpets, Nor is honeyed sleep stripped from the eyelids'; there too sleep is combined with a military metaphor.

11–2   Probably refer to the Roman God of boundaries, Terminus; see Ovid *Fasti* 2.641–2.

14   Probably Silvanus, *aruorum pecorisque deus* according to Virgil *Aeneid* 8.601. He receives offerings of fruit in Horace *Epodes* 2.21–2, a poem which influenced this elegy.

18   A fertility God with a huge phallus. Not a native Italian divinity, he came from Asia Minor via Greece.

20   For the Lares see Introduction p. 16.

27   Sirius rose some days after the summer solstice (Cicero *De Diuinatione* 2.93).

36   Patron Goddess of flocks and herds, whose festival was celebrated on 21 April, the day of Rome's foundation (Cicero *ibid.* 2.98).

53   For Messalla see Introduction p. 14.

67   The Manes, from old Latin *manus* 'good', were the deified spirits of the dead.

2.16   Presupposes the Latin proverb *fortes Fortuna adiuuat* (Cicero *Tusculans* 2.11).

26   Missing in the archetype from which all our MSS derive.

28   Probable allusion to the old Latin word *praemiator* 'robber'.

29–30   The first appearance of the idea that the lover is a sacred person, divinely protected from harm. Tibullus may well have developed it from the Greek epigrammatist Posidippus (*A.P.*5.213): 'Drunk & through thieves have I come, using bold Love as guide'.

35   For the meaning of *parcite luminibus* see Ovid *Metamorphoses* 5.248.

36   Contradicts Catullus 55.20 *uerbosa gaudet Venus loquela*.

41–2   For the birth of Venus-Aphrodite see Hesiod *Theogony* 176–206. Kronos castrated his father Ouranos & threw his genitals into the sea; Aphrodite grew from the foam (*aphros*) that they produced, & when full-grown stepped ashore on the island of Kythera.

53   Medea, the Colchian princess who by her magic enabled Jason to win the Golden Fleece, was for antiquity the prime human example of a sorceress.

54   A formidable Greek Goddess of the Underworld, worshipped by
        witches; she was Medea's patroness (Euripides *Medea* 395); her
        hell-hounds first appear in Apollonius *Argonautica* 3.1217.

2.69   Messalla made an expedition to Cilicia some time after the battle
        of Actium (see 1.7.13–6). The Cilicians were noted for their
        toughness, piracy & saffron.

80   Refers to a fountain playing in the peristyle, or inner court, of
        some wealthy Roman's house.

98   Both among Greeks (Theophrastus *Characters* 16.15) and Romans
        (Pliny *Natural History* 28.35) this was a way of averting bad luck.

3.1–3   For Messalla's expedition to the East see 1.7.13–22. *Cohors* =
        cohors praetoria, the bodyguard & staff of a Roman general.
        Phaeacia was the land of Homer's Phaeacians where Odysseus was
        shipwrecked on his journey home to Ithaca. In the *Odyssey* the
        island is called Scherie; Callimachus *Fragment* 13 identifies it with
        Corcyra, the modern Corfu.

11   Sortilege was a common way among the superstitious of coming
        to a decision. Cicero *De Diuinatione* 2.86 reports that in the temple
        of Fortune at Praeneste the lots were shuffled & drawn *pueri manu*.

18   A reference to the Jewish Sabbath & also evidence that the seven-
        day week was known in the Augustan age (cf. *Corpus Inscriptionum
        Latinarum* 4.6779).

23   The cult of the Egyptian Mother-Goddess Isis, often represented in
        art as a seated Madonna suckling the child Horus, spread through
        the Mediterranean world in the Hellenistic age, reaching Rome in
        the time of Sulla.

28   The pictures, on tablets fixed to the wall, were thank-offerings
        made to the Goddess by those who had recovered from illness &
        other dangers. 'Who does not know that painters are fed by Isis?'
        asks Juvenal at *Satires* 12.28.

32   Pharos, a small island at the entrance to the harbour of Alexandria
        with a famous light-house, was one of the cult centres of Isis.
        Pharian here is used by metonymy (see Quintilian 8.6.23) for
        Egyptian.

35   Saturn was the Roman equivalent of the Greek Kronos & his
        reign was the Golden Age (Hesiod *Erga* 109–20), the *Saturnia regna*
        of Virgil *Eclogue* 4.6.

39–40   Cf. Aratus *Phaenomena* 110–1 (from a description of the Golden
        Age): 'Beyond them lay the cruel sea/and ships were not yet
        bringing livelihood from afar'.

48   Cf. Aratus *ibid.* 108–10: 'Not yet at that time did they know of
        wretched strife/or blameful dissension or the din of battle/but
        simply they lived'.

105   *Explanatory Notes: Book One*

49   Jove (= the Greek Zeus) overcame his father Saturn & reigned in his stead. 'Now' is the Age of Iron (Hesiod *Erga* 176–201).

55–6   It is remarkable that Delia gets no mention in this epitaph, though Messalla does. Contrast Propertius 2.13.35–6.

58   The Elysian 'plain' (*pedion*) first occurs in *Odyssey* 4.563–9. The idea of an Elysium reserved for lovers is perhaps Tibullus's own; so also the substitution of Venus for Mercury as guide of the souls of the departed. More probably Propertius 4.7.59–69 indicates a common source in Greek poetry. The nearest one gets to the description here in surviving Greek poetry is Pindar *Fragments* 129–30, which also has the contrast with Tartarus.

66   Because myrtle is sacred to Venus. I take *insigni* as equivalent to *insignita* here.

67   The Greek Tartaros, equivalent of the Christian Hell.

69   Tisiphone means 'Avenger of Bloodshed' (cf. 49 *caedes*). She is one of the three Erinyes or Furies.

71   The monstrous dog of Hades (Hesiod *Theogony* 311).

72–3   See Pindar *Pythians* 2.21–48.

75   Tityos tried to rape Artemis (*Pythians* 4.90–2).

77   Tantalus raped Ganymede, Jupiter's favourite (Orosius 1.12.4: citing Phanocles' version of the story, a Hellenistic poet).

79   The Danaids murdered their husbands on the wedding night (Aeschylus *Prometheus Vinctus* 853–64).

84–92 For this domestic picture cf. Terence *Heautontimorumenos* 275–307).

94   'The star of Venus which is called *Phosphoros* in Greek, in Latin Lucifer' Cicero *De Natura Deorum* 2.53. The Latin name translates the Greek – 'Light-bringer'.

4.1   For Priapus see 1.1.18 note.

6   Cf. 1.1.27.

7   Priapus was the son of Bacchus & Aphrodite (Pausanias 9.31.2).

21   The first surviving Latin example of the famous commonplace that lovers' perjuries go unpunished.

23–4   Zeus swore falsely to Hera his wife that he had not had intercourse with Io & 'from then on he made the oath without penalty for men, concerning the covert deeds of Cypris' (Hesiod *Fragment* 187). Catullus's friend Calvus had written an epyllion, or short narrative poem in epic hexameters, about Io & there may be a reference to that here.

25–6   Like 23–4 clearly an allusion to some literary context. Dictynna, 'Lady of the Net', was a cult title of Artemis-Diana as Goddess of

the chase. The occurrence of this rare name in a line by Helvius
Cinna – *saecula permaneat nostri Dictynna Catonis* (*Fragment* 14) –
suggests that the reference may be to Valerius Cato's epyllion of
that name.

32   The Olympic Games were held at Elis in the Peloponnese; they
       included horse- as well as chariot-racing.

37–8   Phoebus Apollo is called 'unshorn-haired' (*akersikomes*) at *Iliad*
       20.39, & Dionysus' 'beautiful dark locks are shaken around' at
       Homeric Hymn 7.4–5.

40   Presupposes Virgil *Eclogue* 10.69 *omnia uincit Amor*.

46   The job of a slave, as is also carrying hunting-nets (50).

59–60 Euripides *Hippolytus* 407–9 provides the earliest surviving example
       of the curse on the inventor.

61   *Pierides* was a title of the Muses from Hesiod *Scutum* 206 onwards;
       they were born in Pieria, a district of S.W. Macedonia (Hesiod
       Theogony 54). Tibullus here aligns himself, by implication, with
       the *docti poetae*, a title applied to Catullus and his poet friends. His
       doctrina is evident from the various allusions in this poem & from
       the technical point of this particular couplet.
       See Introduction p.9.

63   Nisus, king of Megara, had a purple lock of hair on which the
       safety of the city depended. His daughter Scylla, in love with the
       enemy commander Minos of Crete, cut off her father's lock &
       betrayed the city to him.

64   Tantalus dismembered his son Pelops & served him up at a banquet
       to the Gods. They were not deceived & reassembled Pelops, apart
       from one shoulder which Ceres had inadvertently eaten & for
       which they provided an ivory replacement.

68–70 Ops, wife of Saturn, is the Roman equivalent of Rhea, wife of
       Kronos. The Greeks identified Rhea with Cybele, the Phrygian
       Mother-Goddess of Mount Ida. Cybele's priests the Galli were
       eunuchs & made a living as wandering beggars. This passage has
       connexions with Callimachus *Fragment* 193.34–6: 'It would be
       more profitable for me (*sc.* than being a poet) to toss my hair for
       Cybele to the sound of the Phrygian flute'.

73   Titius may well be the poet mentioned by Horace in *Epistles* 1.3
       as attempting to write Pindaric Odes in Latin.

79–80 Cf. Callimachus *Fragment* 41: 'That old man ages more lightly
       whom boys love & lead him by the hand to the door of his house
       like their own parent'.

5.8   *Compositum caput* means (i) 'head placed beside mine' cf.
       Propertius 2.14.22, (ii) 'well-groomed head' cf. Virgil *Georgics*

107   *Explanatory Notes: Book One*

4.417, & perhaps (iii) 'heading drawn up' cf. *Oxford Latin Dictionary caput* 17–8.

16 Trivia 'Three-ways' (cf. 56) is the title of Hecate as Goddess of the crossroads & translated from the Greek *Trioditis*. For the identification with Artemis-Diana see Catullus 34.15.

35 On the analogy of *Iliad* 2.145–6 'the waves which Eurus & Notus has raised' i.e. Euronotus, the S.E. wind.

45–6 Haemonia was the old name for Thessaly, Haemon being the father of Thessalus. Peleus, king of Phthia, in Thessaly, by the will of Zeus married the sea-goddess Thetis, who was fated to produce a son greater than his father: that son was Achilles. Catullus wrote an epyllion about the wedding (Poem 64).

49–50 Cf. Callimachus *Fragment* 530 'Flesh like to gall may you eat'. The *deuotiones*, or flyting, in 49–56 can be thought of as arising from *deuotum* in 41; they represent the poet's answer to the bawd, who is also a witch (59).

52 Pliny in *Natural History* 11.232 is not sure what bird this is, but Ovid knows it is an owl that screeches horribly & sucks the blood of children (*Fasti* 6.131–42).

64 For the probable secondary meaning cf. Ovid *Amores* 1.4.57–8 *agmine me inuenies aut inuenieris in illo;/quicquid ibi poteris tangere, tange, mei.*

66 Sandals were not worn during a Roman dinner, cf. Horace *Satires* 2.8.77.

76 For the ending with a disconnected proverb cf. 1.2.98.

6.22 A Roman fertility Goddess whose cult was confined to women. Her annual celebration was held in December in the house of a magistrate with *imperium* & presided over by his wife assisted by the Vestal Virgins. In 60 B.C. there had been a famous scandal when Clodius dressed up as a woman & took part in her rites.

24 The allusion is to blindness as the penalty for profanation. The implication is either that Delia is a greater goddess than the Bona Dea or, more likely, that the poet would be in no danger of seeing her with another man.

37–8 The girl's *custos* would be a slave & liable to these punishments if he failed in his duty.

39–40 Dandies, like the young men round Catiline as Cicero describes them: *pexo capillo . . . uelis amictos, non togis* (*Catilines* 2.22).

45 The Roman Goddess of War, whose temple was in the Campus Martius. Her worshippers were notorious for their religious frenzy, e.g. Juvenal 4.123–4 *fanaticus oestro/percussus, Bellona, tuo.*

67–8 See Introduction p.14.

7.1   The Parcae were the Roman equivalent of the Greek Moirai, or
Fates, who according to Plato *Republic* 617 & Catullus 64. 306 ff.
sang as they spun the thread of destiny.

3   These tribes occupied the area from Pyrenees to Garonne (Caesar
Gallic War 1.1); for the names of most of them see Caesar *ibid.*
3.27.

4   The MSS give *Atax*, the modern Aude, which was well inside the
Roman province of Gallia Narbonensis. Had the Aquitani invaded
the province & crossed the Atax it is hard to believe that its
recovery by Messalla would have been referred to like this.
Therefore read *Atur* with Scaliger; for the form see Vibius
Sequester (Riese) p. 146. The Atur, modern Adour, was in the
territory of the Tarbelli in S.W. Aquitania.

9–12   Messalla's operations must have taken place in an area bounded by
Pyrenees in S, Loire in N, Bay of Biscay in W, Saône & upper
Rhone in E. The Santoni (hence modern Saintonge & Saintes)
were a Celtic tribe between Charente & Garonne (Caesar *Gallic
War* 1.10); the Carnutes (hence Chartres) a Celtic tribe between
Seine & Loire. Messalla's Triumph *ex Gallia* is firmly dated by the
Fasti Consulares to 25 September 27 B.C.

13   A Cilician river rising in Mt Taurus & flowing through Tarsus.

18   The dove was sacred to the Syrian Goddess Astarte (Lucian *De
Syria Dea* 54).

27   Osiris was brother & husband of Isis & identified by the
Egyptians with the Nile (Plutarch *Isis* 33).

28   Apis, the sacred bull of Memphis. The line adapts Callimachus
Fragment 383.16 (also a pentameter) 'knowing to keen the lucent
bull'.

39   The Greeks identified Osiris with Dionysus-Bacchus (Herodotus
2.42).

49   The Genius was each man's guardian spirit: 'The companion who
tempers the star of our birth, the God of human nature, subject
to death in each individual life' (Horace *Epistles* 2.2.187–9).
According to Censorinus *De Die Natali* 3, he was identified with
the Lar by many.

51   Cf. Callimachus *Fragment* 7.12 'And unguent from your ringlets
ever flows'.

54   Callimachus referred to Attica as Mopsopia (*Fragment* 709).

57–8   Between Tusculum & the Alban Mount ran the Via Latina. The
Feriae Latinae were held annually on the Alban Mount & would
draw crowds.
Combination of lines 57–60 with Suetonius *Augustus* 30 allows us to
infer that Messalla paid for the repair of this stretch of the Via

109   *Explanatory Notes: Book One*

Latina with money brought in by the sale of booty from his
Gallic campaign.

63   Natalis, the Birthday Spirit, was probably identical with the
the Genius; cf. 3.12.1 *Natalis Iuno* – a woman's Genius was called
her Juno.

8.3–4   The reference is to three kinds of divination: sortilege, haruspicy
(examination of entrails), augury (observation of the flight & call of
birds). *Fibra* is a division or lobe of the liver.

5–6   Venus treats the lover like a slave. For the form of the sentence cf.
Callimachus *Fragment* 67.1 'Eros himself taught Akontios . . .'

10   Cf. Callimachus *Hymn* 5.22 'Many-times-twice she altered the
same hair'.

19   Cf. Virgil *Eclogue* 8.99. The Twelve Tables specified a punishment
for the person *qui fruges excantassit* (Pliny *Natural History* 28.17).

21–2   Cf. Virgil *Eclogue* 8.70. Bronze instruments were clashed and
banged to frighten the demons responsible for the moon's eclipse:
see Gow on Theocritus 2.36.

31–2   Cf. Theocritus 15.130 'The kiss does not prickle; golden down is
still about his lips' (of Adonis).

35–8   I take as an allusion to the love of Venus for the young Adonis;
cf. the Theocritean passage quoted at 31–2 above.

44   The green outer skin of the walnut (Pliny *Natural History* 15.87).

46   Pliny mentions mastic gum (*N.H.* 24–43); Juvenal a dough plaster
(6.462).

9.24–8   It is not clear who this mysterious God is; perhaps Amor.

33   Noted for its fertility; cf. Pliny *N.H.* 3.60 *felix illa Campania*.

34   Cf. Isidore *Etymologiae* 20.3.6 *Falernum uinum uocatum a Falerna
regione Campaniae, ubi optima uina nascuntur.*

37   Cf. Callimachus 193.30 (same situation) 'I was honourably
educated'.

42   The job of a slave.

47   For the full meaning of *attonita* see *Oxford Latin Dictionary
attonitus* 2(c) 'spellbound', 3 'inspired' & 4 'crazy'.

83   The possibility of taking *fallaci* with *tibi* is difficult to reproduce in
English; I have done my best.

10.1–2   A variant of the curse on the inventor: cf. 1.4.59–60 note. The
existing phrase *ferus et ferreus*, already found in Cicero *Ad Quintum
Fratrem* 1.3.31, is given fresh point in the ferrous context.

7–8   Cf. Plato *Phaedo* 66c 'It is in order to get money that all wars are
made'.

10   Spotted fleeces were bad (Varro *Res Rusticae* 2.2.4). In primitive
        days we are to suppose the profit motive did not operate & there
        were neither sheep-breeders nor sheep-thieves; spotted was as good
        as pure white.

11   The emendation *Valgi* is uncertain. Anyhow, C. Valgius Rufus,
        who later held the consulship in 12 B.C., was a writer of elegies
        whose judgement of poetry Horace respected (*Satires* 1.10.82) &
        who is praised as an epic poet at [Tibullus] 3.4.181. Two pastoral
        hexameters of his are quoted by a scholiast on Virgil *Georgic*
        3.177; their tone is in harmony with this elegy.

25–6   A pentameter & a hexameter must have been missing in the
        archetype between these two lines.

36   The sound of the adjective *audax*, emphatically placed at the line-
        ending, suggests barking in this context. The *nauita* is Charon, who
        on payment of an obolus ferried the dead man's spirit across the
        river Styx.

39–40   The contrast is with those *qui militari laude antecellunt* (Cicero
        Pro Murena 24). Cf. 1.1.57 *non ego laudari curo*. *Piger* is a word of
        military disapproval (see Lewis & Short).

43   Perhaps as opposed to the warrior *aere caput fulgens* (Virgil *Aeneid*
        10.869).

44   Contrasts with 31.

49–50   Cf. Bacchylides *Fragment* 4.31–4 (in praise of Peace): 'On the iron-
        bound handles of shields are shining spiders' webs. Rust
        overpowers sharp-pointed spears & two-edged swords'. And cf.
        1.1.4 note.

51   A couplet has probably dropped out after 50. Perhaps there was a
        hole in the archetype between 25 and 26 on the recto side of the
        skin & the hole on the verso was between 50 & 51. The position of
        que in 51 is odd: exceptionally late to connect this sentence with
        what precedes; on the other hand *rusticus* as running on from a
        missing pentameter would be equally exceptional; perhaps
        hyperbaton for *uxoremque*?

53–64   There is probably a criticism of this passage in Propertius
        2.5.21–6, as Solmsen has argued in *Philologus* 105 (1961) 273 ff.
        This enables one to date the publication of Tibullus's first book
        between 25 September 27 B.C., the date of Messalla's triumph, and
        25 B.C., the probable date of Propertius 2.

BOOK TWO

The first elegy begins with a poetic dramatisation (on the analogy
of Callimachus *Hymn* 5) of the *lustratio agri* or purification of the

land, referred to by Cato *De Agri Cultura* 141. The ritual circumambulation of the fields has a parallel, perhaps a remote continuation, in the Rogation ceremonies of the Christian Church.

1.27–8   It was believed that smoke in moderation matured wine more quickly (Columella *De Re Rustica* 1.6.20). The Chian would be mixed with the Falernian (cf. Horace *Satires* 1.10.24).

34   According to Varro the Romans started shaving in 300 BC (Pliny *Natural History* 11.211).

49   Strangely enough from Aristotle onwards classical writers assert that bees carry flowers. See Gow on Theocritus 7.81.

55–8   There seems to be a fusion here of the Aristotelian theory of tragedy's origin in the dithyramb (*Poetics* 1449a) & the later idea that the name tragedy arose because a goat (*tragos*) was the prize for the best singing (*ode*). See Brink on Horace *Ars Poetica* 220.

66   The weights which keep the warp tight are made of brick (*later*).

67–8   The first mention of this tradition, which re-appears in *Peruigilium Veneris* 77 *ipse Amor puer Dionae rure natus creditur*.

87–8   Cf. Aeschylus *Choephori* 660 'Hurry, for Night's dark chariot hastens on' & Theocritus 2.166 'The stars that follow still Night's wheel'.

2.1   For Natalis see 1.7.63 note.

5   For the Genius see 1.7.49 note. Presumably the image of the Genius would be carried from the Lararium to the scene of the birthday ceremonies. The nodding in line 10 would then not be pure fantasy; cf. Ovid *Amores* 3.2.58 where the statue of Venus is being carried in procession & a tilt of the head is taken as a nod.

17   Text & interpretation uncertain; I have chosen the one that gives some point to *strepitantibus*.

18   For saffron or yellow as a colour connected with marriage see Catullus 61.8–10 where the Marriage-God wears the *flammeum* or flame-coloured veil of the bride & yellow slippers.

21   Text & interpretation uncertain; I have chosen the one that gives most point to *auis*.

3.11*ff.*   This is by far the longest of the very few mythological illustrations in the work of Tibullus & clearly has a Greek poetical source behind it. One notices the Alexandrian treatment (Apollo's love for Admetus is first mentioned in Callimachus *Hymn* 2.49) exploiting paradox & incongruity & describing the technique of cheese-making in detail (cf. the detailed description of spinning in Catullus 64.311–9). Line 16, & perhaps a couplet after that, was missing in the archetype.

112

28   Juno was Apollo's stepmother (*nouerca*).

31   Delos, the island where Apollo was born, & Delphi were the chief
      centres of his cult; Pytho was the name of the district round
      Delphi.

37–8 Addressee & situation are obscure, so one assumes that at least one
      couplet has fallen out after line 38.

51–2 Samian & Cumaean ware was elegant but relatively inexpensive.
      There is probably another lacuna hereabouts, for this couplet seems
      oddly disconnected, though the translation glosses this over.

64   Slaves on sale from abroad had their feet coated with chalk as a
      distinguishing mark (Pliny *Natural History* 35.199). When on the
      platform in the market they would have to mark time at the
      double to prove their physical fitness to prospective buyers.

75   Cf. Apollonius *Argonautica* 3.936–7 'On thee neither Cypris (i.e.
      Venus) nor the gentle Loves breathe friendly'.

79   The hexameter was missing from the archetype.

82   This line may perhaps have given rise to *cultuque corporis
      obseruabilis* in the *Vita Tibulli*, for a *toga laxa* was the sign of a
      dandy; see 1.6.39–40 n.

4.17–8 I.e. didactic poetry such as the *Phaenomena* of Aratus.

20   Plays on the other meaning of *carmina*, 'incantations'.

33–4 Cf. Antipater of Thessalonica (*Anthologia Palatina* 5.30.3–4) 'For if
      you bring the coin, friend, no keeper stands in the way, no dog is
      chained at the front-door'. Gow & Page date this epigram as later
      than Tibullus, however.

55   Circe is the divine witch of the *Odyssey*, who turned Odysseus'
      comrades into swine. For Medea see 1.2.53 note.

56   Cf. Apuleius *Metamorphoses* 2.1: 'Thessaly, celebrated by the
      concordant voice of all the globe as birthplace of the magic art's
      cantillations.'

58   For more about mares & *hippomanes*, the reputed aphrodisiac first
      mentioned by Aristotle, see Virgil *Georgic* 3.266–83.

5   In this his longest & most ambitious elegy Tibullus celebrates the
      induction of Messalla's son Messallinus into the priestly college of
      fifteen members known as the *Quindecimuiri*; it was the duty of
      this college to guard the Sibylline Books & to consult them when
      the Senate thought fit. There is inscriptional evidence for
      Messallinus as the junior member of the college in 17 B.C. (*Corpus
      Inscriptionum Latinarum* 6.32323.152).

5.1–10 Tibullus probably has in mind the statue of Apollo Citharoedus by
      Scopas (4th century B.C.) which Augustus had placed in his temple

of Apollo on the Palatine (Pliny *Natural History* 36.25 & Suetonius *Augustus* 29).

9–10   See notes on 1.3.35 & 49.

15–16   The Sibyl of Cumae who sold the original Sibylline Books of oracles in Greek hexameter verse to Tarquin the Proud (see Lactantius *Diuinae Institutiones* 1.6.10 & 13).

19–22   The Sibyl's prophecy of Aeneas begins at line 39; in between comes a long parenthesis on the early site of Rome, perhaps derived from Varro's *Antiquitates*.

24   Romulus killed Remus for insulting him by jumping over the wall of his new city (Livy 1.7).

27–8   The Greek nature God Pan was identified with the Latin Silvanus, referred to as *siluestri deo* in line 30. For Pales see 1.1.36 note.

33   The Velabrum lay between Palatine & Tiber.

39   Both Aeneas & Cupid were sons of Venus.

41   Aeneas landed at Laurentum, a few miles below Ostia.

43   The Numicus (modern Rio Torto) runs into the sea between Ostia & Anzio.

47–8   Turnus, chief of the Rutuli, fought Aeneas for the bride Lavinia whom King Latinus, her father, had previously promised to him.

50   Ascanius alias Iulus was Aeneas's son.

52   Ilia was the mother of Romulus & Remus by Mars. The priestesses of Vesta, Roman Goddess of the Hearth, had to be virgins; their duty was to keep the sacred fire in her temple burning.

It has been maintained that lines 39–54 imply knowledge of Virgil's *Aeneid* on the part of Tibullus. This is unlikely for the following reasons: (i) the *Aeneid* does not associate the death & deification of Aeneas with the river Numicus; (ii) there is no mention in the *Aeneid* of a fire in the Rutulian camp; (iii) the story of Ilia is referred to at *Aeneid* 1.273–4 but Tibullus's version has details that derive from another source.

61   Rome was New Troy.

67–70   The list of Sibyls probably derives from Varro, who is quoted by Lactantius in *Diuinae Institutiones* 1.6.

71–8   Describe the portents following the murder of Julius Caesar, doing in elegiacs what Virgil had done on a grander scale in hexameters at *Georgic* 1.466–88.

87   For the Palilia see 1.1.36 note.

116   In the Latin the *praemia belli* are conquered towns because floats representing the towns took part in the triumphal procession.

114

6.1 This may be the Pompeius Macer to whom Ovid addresses
    Amores 2.6 & *Ex Ponto* 2.10.

19–20 Cf. Theocritus 4.41–2 'Cheer up, friend Battus. Perhaps tomorrow
    will be better. There's hope for the living; only the dead have
    none.'

25–6 Slaves were sometimes sent as a punishment to work on the land in
    chain-gangs, a practice which Pliny in *Natural History* 18.36
    deplores.

45 *Phryne* is the Greek word for toad.

THE EPITAPH

In the 1570s Scaliger had access to a fragmentary MS, now lost,
which began at 3.4.65; in it this epigram was attributed to
Domitius Marsus.
Line 2 refers to 1.3.58.

THE LIFE

Suetonian parallels are as follows: *Nero* 20.3 *insignes . . . coma*;
Julius 45.3 *cultu notabilem*, 50.2 *ante alias dilexit*, 42.1 *contubernalis*;
Augustus 8.1 *militaribus donis . . . donatus est*; *De Grammaticis* 23.1
principem locum inter grammaticos tenuit; *Nero* 57.1 *obiit*; *De
Grammaticis* 16 *quod etiam uersiculus Domiti Marsi indicat*. For
elegiographos cf. the parallel formation *mimographos* in *De
Grammaticis* 18.

  The 'amatory epistles' are usually taken to be poems 8–12 in
Book 3, though in fact there is nothing to indicate that these
poems are letters; they are short elegies, like 2.2, or epigrams;
moreover, echoes of Ovid's *Metamorphoses* & *Fasti* prove that they
cannot be the work of Tibullus. It seems more likely that the
epistles in question have not survived.

CHRONOLOGICAL GUIDE

?55   Birth of Tibullus. Death of Lucretius.

?54   Death of Catullus.

53   Crassus defeated by the Parthians at Carrhae.

49   Caesar crosses the Rubicon.

48   Caesar defeats Pompey at Pharsalus.

45   Cicero *Tusculan Disputations*.

44   Murder of Caesar. Cicero *De Officiis*.

43   Birth of Ovid. Murder of Cicero.

42   Antony & Octavian defeat Brutus & Cassius at Philippi. Messalla surrenders to Antony.

40   Pollio's consulship. Virgil *Eclogue* 4.

?38   Virgil *Eclogues*. Gallus *Amores* published by this date.

?35   Horace *Satires* I.

31   Messalla's consulship. Octavian defeats Antony at Actium.

30   Horace *Epodes* & *Satires* II.

?29   Virgil *Georgics*. Propertius I.

27   Octavian receives title of Augustus. Messalla's Triumph. Death of Varro.

?26   Tibullus I.

?25   Propertius II.

?23   Horace *Odes* I–III. ?First edition of Ovid *Amores* I.

?21   Propertius III.

20   Settlement with Parthia.

19   Death of Virgil. Horace *Epistles* I.

?18   Death of Tibullus. Publication of Tibullus II.

SELECT BIBLIOGRAPHY

DISSEN, L. *Tibulli Carmina*, Göttingen, 1835 (reprinted Hildesheim, 1969).

HARRAUER, H. *A Bibliography to the Corpus Tibullianum*, Hildesheim, 1971.

LENZ, F. W., & GALINSKY, G. C. *Albii Tibulli aliorumque carminum libri tres*, Leiden, 1971.

LUCK, G. *The Latin Love Elegy*, London, 2nd edition 1969.

POSTGATE, J. P. *Selections from Tibullus*, London, 2nd edition revised 1922.

PUTNAM, M. C. J. *Tibullus: a Commentary*, Oklahoma, 1973.

SMITH, K. F. *The Elegies of Albius Tibullus*, New York, 1913 (reprinted Darmstadt, 1964).

BULLOCH, A. W. 'Tibullus & the Alexandrians', *Proceedings of the Cambridge Philological Society* n.s.19 (1973) 71–89.